War Heroes

WAR HEROES

*True Stories of
Congressional
Medal of Honor
Recipients*

KENT DeLONG

PRAEGER

Westport, Connecticut
London

Library of Congress Cataloging-in-Publication Data

DeLong, Kent.
    War heroes : true stories of Congressional Medal of Honor recipients /
Kent DeLong.
        p.   cm.
    ISBN 0–275–94309–7 (alk. paper)
    1. Medal of Honor.   2. United States—Armed Forces—Biography.
I. Title.
    UB433.D45   1993
    355.1′342′092273—dc20   92–39283
    [B]

British Library Cataloguing in Publication Data is available.

Library of Congress Catalog Card Number: 92–39283
ISBN: 0–275–94309–7

First published in 1993

Praeger Publishers, 88 Post Road West, Westport, CT 06881
An imprint of Greenwood Publishing Group, Inc.

Printed in the United States of America

The paper used in this book complies with the
Permanent Paper Standard issued by the National
Information Standards Organization (Z39.48–1984).

10 9 8 7 6 5 4 3 2 1

Somewhere, sometime, in unknown and unrecorded incidents of combat, heroes worthy as those described in this book have fallen in battles where they believed that more than their own lives were at risk. Because their sacrifices were not seen, their deeds are not known.

Medal of Honor recipient Elliott Williams once said, "I know there are men who have fought desperately in battle with a complete disregard for their own personal safety—soldiers who were not recognized for their commitment and sacrifice simply because their actions were not observed and recorded. These men are my heroes."

They are mine too. Unsung, unknown but only to God . . . we owe you much. To you brave men this book is dedicated.

War is an ugly thing, but not the ugliest of things; the decayed and degraded state of moral and patriotic feeling which thinks nothing is worth war is much worse.

A man who has nothing for which he is willing to fight, nothing he cares about more than his own personal safety, is a miserable creature who has no chance of being free, unless made and kept so by exertions of better men than himself.

—Art Cavagnaro, USMC (ret.)

CONTENTS

x   Contents

INTRODUCTION

The history of the United States is a record of heroes who sacrificed to build this nation's greatness. A few of these people received the highest honor this country can give, the Congressional Medal of Honor.

The Medal of Honor is awarded by the president to soldiers. These soldiers—most killed during their actions—conspicuously distinguished themselves above and beyond the call of their duty while engaged in action against an enemy of the United States.

The deeds recognized for the Medal of Honor are ones of personal bravery or self-sacrifice so conspicuous that the action is clearly more than what could ever have been expected. The action must involve significant risk of life and be done without any thought by the individual soldier for future reward.

Once recommended for the Medal of Honor by eyewitnesses, the soldier's action is painstakingly verified and reviewed. The event must be documented so that absolutely no doubt about its accuracy can exist. This review process is conducted at the highest levels of the military and is so strict that fewer than two hundred recipients of this award are alive today.

The award has been received by people from all walks of life. These people have come from every state, from every branch of military service, and from many different religions and races. Some were poor and some were rich; some were educated and some were not. Yet they all had in common the belief that an ideal—their country—or even just another person was more important than their own life. And then, with courage and sacrifice, they acted.

These actions must never be forgotten.

The men described in the following pages have shown their willingness to make the ultimate sacrifice for the good of others. These men may have little more in common than this willingness. But this—along with uncommon dedication, courage, and honor—is the definition of a true hero, a Congressional Medal of Honor recipient.

War Heroes

Part I

AIR

1.

LEO K. THORSNESS

Wearing It Humbly

Sometimes, the personal character of a Medal of Honor recipient is seen better during unrelated actions. Leo Thorsness may be one of these. Shot down eleven days after his "Medal Day," Thorsness showed endurance and inner strength through terrible conditions few people have ever experienced. As proven during the six and a half years he was a prisoner in the "Hanoi Hilton," sacrifice and honor are more than just words to Leo Thorsness.

Leo K. Thorsness
Major, U.S. Air Force
Over North Vietnam
19 April 1967

Leo Thorsness flew Wild Weasels.

An experienced jet pilot, he went to Vietnam in 1966 to do one of the toughest and most dangerous jobs in the Air Force: surface-to-air missile (SAM) hunting.

Born in Walnut Grove, Minnesota, flying came easy for Thorsness and he loved his job. He remembers, "It's hard to believe the military would put you in a state-of-the-art fighter jet and actually pay you to fly it. It's the world's best job. It was like giving a kid a Porsche and a credit card."

By the time Thorsness arrived in Vietnam he had a family, a Master's degree, and more than three thousand hours flying jets. He knew his job.

The Wild Weasel airplanes were two-place F-105s, which were as big as the old B-17 bombers. They could go twice the speed of sound, and they lived to kill the enemy's SAM launch sites so the U.S. bombers wouldn't get shot down. As a result, Weasels were shot down more than any other airplanes in Vietnam. In fact, by the time Thorsness and his "backseater" and close friend Harry Johnson arrived at their new home—the Tak-hil Air Force Base in Thailand—no Weasel had ever completed a full hundred-mission tour!

Thorsness did his job well and actually started thinking he might make the hundred missions in time to go home by Mother's Day. Thorsness remembers his eighty-fifth mission: "We were hitting a military barracks complex on the delta about thirty miles southeast of Hanoi. There was usually a lot of flak and SAMs in this area."

As the Weasels approached the target, a "fan song" radar signal appeared, which told them a SAM site had seen them. Thorsness's wingman in the other plane, Tom Madison, let go a SHRIKE missile that killed the site. Another site showed, and

Thorsness dropped a cluster bomb, destroying that one too. As they were pulling off, Thorsness's wingman picked up some flak and reported, "Leo, I have fire warning lights!" The wingman was behind and Thorsness couldn't see his plane. He ordered, "Guard your channel and head for the hills."

Madison yelled into the radio, "There are more things going wrong in this cockpit. Leo, I'm getting out." Thorsness could hear one of their parachute beepers go off, and then the second one. Both pilots had ejected from their failing plane.

By now, everyone else from the mission was out of the area. Thorsness remembers, "We were the only plane left and there were SAMs all over the place. I saw those parachutes going down, and then I picked up a MIG starting to roll in on them." Thorsness immediately engaged the enemy jet, and a short fierce fight ended its flight. Then Johnson called from the backseat, "We have four more MIGs on our ass!" Thorsness turned around and looked back: sure enough, there was a "wagon wheel" of MIGS on their tail.

An F-105 was built like a sled. It could go as fast as any airplane in the world; it just couldn't turn as well. Thorsness dropped down and started screaming up a valley at supersonic speed. "That's kind of exciting when you're only twenty feet above the ground," Thorsness recalls. "We outran the MIGs, but by now we were low on fuel."

Thorsness went back up and found a tanker plane to get fuel. He started calling for fighters to help with the rescue and found none available. By now, there were two rescue aircraft—the "SANDYs"—going into the area with no support. Thorsness and Johnson made their decision: "Let's go back in."

Observers later described the scene: "It looked like Leo and Harry decided to take on the entire North Vietnamese Air Force by themselves." There were enemy planes and missiles in the area, and flak was everywhere.

As they headed back in, SANDY 2 came on the radio and excitedly reported, "SANDY 1 is going in." The MIGs had found the rescue aircraft; the lead searcher was shot and going down.

Then, SANDY 2 came back on and yelled, "I have four MIGs on me." It was kind of like, "What should I do now?" Leo remembers. "They can't turn with you," Leo instructed. "Turn hard and stay low! I'll be there shortly." Thorsness fired his afterburners and started racing to get back to the area from the refueling tanker.

As he approached the area, Thorsness saw a MIG right at his altitude. There were no clouds and it was just getting dark. He needed about two thousand feet and got it; then, with a slight turn toward the MIG, he started to "hose" it. The enemy plane came apart.

By now, Thorsness was out of ammunition. He homed in on the remaining SANDY and saw the MIGs: they were all around him. Thorsness remembers, "I figured it would be better to have MIGs chase us than him." So he raced down into the middle of the enemy jets and whispered to himself, "Come get me." Sure enough, a couple of them did and Thorsness started to run away with them on his tail.

Finally, just in time, a flight of four F-4 fighters came in. They quickly attacked the enemy MIGs, shooting one down. The rest scattered, and SANDY 2 was saved. The men in SANDY 1 were killed; Thorsness's downed wingmen ended up getting captured. "I was sick about losing those men," Thorsness recalls. "We hung it out and should have been shot down too. But we were lucky."

That day, Thorsness shot down two enemy airplanes and eventually received his country's highest award—the Medal of Honor—for his heroism on this mission. Johnson would receive the second highest award: the Distinguished Flying Cross. But neither man knew about these honors for more than six years because of what happened eleven days later, when they flew their ninety-third mission.

Thorsness remembers, "I had flown a mission that morning. On this second mission, they needed pilots, so Harry and I went." Thorsness left at noon, but he wasn't very well briefed. "I had a feeling this wasn't such a good idea."

It was actually supposed to be a relatively light mission over some foothills west of Hanoi. Thorsness remembers, "We were up there traveling at six hundred knots about forty miles from Hanoi and everything seemed routine." The Weasels started to pull up to their target when Johnson in the backseat reported, "Air to air painting!" This meant that a missile had been launched at them from another aircraft somewhere. Thorsness demanded, "What's the position?" An F-4 support fighter following Thorsness's airplane calmly answered, "We're at your six o'clock, Weasel. You're clear."

Then Thorsness was blown out of the air.

Two MIGs had pulled up from hiding in a mountain valley and hosed off their Russian Sidewinders at Thorsness and his wingman. "Those sledgehammers blew right up our tailpipes," Thorsness remembers. "Our rudders flopped and the engines blew." The smoke was so thick in the cockpit that, even with his face shield pressed against the canopy, Thorsness couldn't see out. He yelled, "Harry, go!" Johnson responded with "Shit," and ejected. Thorsness followed. The other airplane was tumbling out of control, but eventually the wingman was able to grab the handles and squeeze his ejection trigger too. Thorsness didn't see him again for three years.

"When I hit the airstream at six hundred miles an hour, it was like hitting a wall. I could feel my knees rip outward and my legs did the splits. My helmet was blown right off and when the chute opened about a quarter of the panels ripped out." Looking down, Thorsness could see a small clearing in the jungle. He could also see muzzle flashes from rifles being fired up at him. He had only two thoughts. First, how was his family going to take this? And second, he knew he wouldn't be rescued. He could see Harry's chute coming down in the distance.

When he landed, Thorsness couldn't walk. His knees were badly torn on the inside from being blown apart by the airstream during the ejection. He started crawling up a hill. And then he heard them coming. When he saw the enemy soldiers, they were just kids—about twenty teenagers. A couple of them had rifles, but mostly they had sticks and machetes.

"They seemed afraid of me. They tied my arms back and put a black bag over my head. The last thing I saw was a machete being pointed at me and pulled back. I imagined, right into my stomach, this was it. Again it flashed to me, how would my wife and kid ever know what happened to me? I realized my biggest disappointment was they would never know. But, I didn't die."

Thorsness was stripped of his clothes and boots. He couldn't walk, so the Vietnamese started beating him. Finally, the captors cut a net and put it on poles for Thorsness to be carried. Four of them started carrying him down the hill. By now, Thorsness was totally exhausted and actually fell asleep in the net. It was about three o'clock in the afternoon.

They traveled down the mountain and into the night until they arrived at an open building with a thatch roof. It was built on stilts and made of bamboo. By now it was pitch dark, and Thorsness was put inside the building. Ten minutes later, Johnson arrived. Thorsness was happy to see his partner and friend. It felt good to be together again. The prisoners were surrounded by squatting old men smoking opium pipes, who were deciding what to do with them.

Thorsness said to his partner, "I think we're having a trial. There is some likelihood we'll be executed tonight." Johnson's answer was simple but profound, "They either are or they aren't, but it's no use to worry about it."

Later that night, Thorsness's captors put him back in his net and started to travel again. About daybreak, they put the prisoners in a jail of sorts. It was a ten-by-twelve-foot cell. Thorsness and Johnson were told not to talk with each other.

The Vietnamese started to interrogate the prisoners separately, in a pigpen. One time Johnson hollered to his partner from the pigpen, "Don't give in, Leo!" He was beaten for this.

Thorsness began learning how to walk with two sticks. He

found he could walk pigeon-toed with his knees turned in. That night, they had to walk to a truck about three hundred yards and one hundred angry people away. A crowd was lining both sides of the path, ready to beat the prisoners when they went by. As the pilots began making their way to the truck, the mob started beating and spitting on them.

First they hit Johnson—which warmed them up for Thorsness. When the prisoners got about fifty yards from the truck, the crowd went out of control. The guards, who at first were encouraging the crowd, started getting scared. There was a big reward for bringing in a captured American pilot. "I think maybe someone might have started worrying about that reward," Thorsness suggests.

The mob beat Thorsness to the ground. They took his walking sticks away and he started to crawl. The guards tried to hold the people back. "I would have given odds I wouldn't make it. Those people were out of control," Thorsness remembers.

Finally the prisoners made it to the truck, which then sped away from the mob. The pilots were told that if they talked they would be hit. Still, Thorsness and Johnson would make quick comments just to reassure each other and tell each other they were still together. "Everything okay, Harry?" "Yea, what about you, Leo?" Then they would get hit.

"The Hanoi Hilton was a big, gray, dirty building," Thorsness remembers. "You are about to enter prison and you have hopes you will meet up with some nice prison guard and you could be buddies. But you know this isn't going to happen." It didn't.

The guards met the truck and pushed Thorsness down a dirty dark corridor into a small room. An interrogator came in. Thorsness stood as erect as he could, using the wall to lean against. Saluting, he gave his name, rank, and date of birth. The interrogator glared at him, knocked him to the floor, and said, "You are no longer in the military."

Thorsness's interrogation began. And eventually in this kind of interrogation—whether it took only hours or whether it took days—all prisoners either broke down or died. "I still have bad dreams when I talk about this," Thorsness remembers. "They tortured me or they shackled me in the stocks for eighteen straight days and nights. You can't stay awake that long. By the end of the interrogation, I was in a state where I would answer any question they asked."

The Vietnamese knew how to make a suitcase out of the prisoners. They would strap them down and pull their elbows back until the shoulder joints dislocated out of their sockets. Then they would put the men in stocks that had half-moons for the feet with level bars across the top just like in the cartoons. But there was no humor here: the stocks were always too tight, and they would squeeze the open sores on the prisoner's legs until the pus ran out.

Thorsness began developing the ability to hallucinate at will. As he says, "I guess when the body hurts so bad, the mind detaches. It was a nice escape to hallucinate. I could talk to anybody I wanted to." Sometimes these "discussions" upset Thorsness because life was always going very well for everyone he talked to. Things weren't going so well for him.

After the heartbreaking nightmare of interrogation, Thorsness went to a regular cell. But the treatment of him didn't improve much. There were still frequent beatings, little food, cold and wet living facilities, and every kind of abuse. "One time, I stood in the middle of my cell and asked God to have the walls come down; then I marched a circle in the cell seven times just like at Jericho. The walls didn't fall. I guess I really didn't expect them too . . . but it would have been nice."

One time, at the edge of a six-foot cement slab in the middle of his cell, Thorsness felt a small cross that someone had left. After he found it, he had a very difficult time letting it go. It seemed to give him hope, just to touch it. Because the guards would have taken it away, Thorsness left the cross under the slab. Symbolically, it became a source of strength to him, and he would often keep his hand on the cross while lying face down on the floor of his cell.

Initially, the prisoners lived with two people in their small cells. But later the guards identified thirty-six "troublemakers," and Thorsness was one of them. He was taken out of his regular cell and put on "skid row." These were six-by-six foot cells. Every other day, the guards would pour some water for the prisoners and let them out for about five minutes. Thorsness stayed here for a year.

"When they strip you of everything, all you have left is what's inside you," Thorsness recalls. "I took a vow that, if life is going to mean anything, it should mean it here in solitary confinement. For the rest of my life, I promised to find something to enjoy every day, and I have."

Because the prisoners would often be beaten if they talked, a good part of prisoner communication was from a soft tap code on the walls. They couldn't use Morse code because you couldn't do dashes by tapping on walls. So the prisoners turned the alphabet into a code that consisted of five rows of letters across and five columns of letters down, totaling twenty-five letters. "K" was eliminated; "C" was used for it. The prisoners would tap which row the letter was in—one through five— followed by which column it was in, and they got very good and very fast at this.

The prisoners tried to memorize as much of what everyone else knew as they could. Thorsness memorized all forty-eight verses of the "Ballad of East and West." He learned the full names of all 350 prisoners. He memorized the Twenty-third Psalm and he learned the capitals of all the states. He even learned the names of all the presidents, in chronological order. Thorsness got to the point where he would spend a couple of hours each day reciting to himself the things he memorized.

"I learned the Beautitudes were written just for Vietnam POWs," Thorsness recalls. "There's something in those words that applies to every tough time or every struggle. They were very appropriate for those of us in Hanoi."

The prisoners taught courses to each other. Thorsness taught a real estate course, and once he spent a day teaching the prisoners how to milk a cow. They would teach each other foreign languages—and if they didn't know a certain word, they would make one up.

They even started their own Toastmaster's Club. The prisoner with the most regular pulse each day was the speech timer. When they came home later, they actually applied for an American Toastmaster's charter and got one for the "Hanoi Branch."

Certain traditions developed in prison. When a new pilot came in, the other prisoners exchanged torture stories just once, and then they didn't talk about it again.

Another tradition was the "POW Fact." This was a story that could either be the truth or a lie: accuracy wasn't important. It just had to be a story with a happy ending.

From their captors, the prisoners received the Vietnamese version of the news. They were told about floods, riots, and plane crashes. The entire text of the Pentagon Papers was read to them three times. They heard much about the war protestors and, in fact, repeatedly heard Jane Fonda's assurance to the world that they were being treated well.

They would find things to smile about, like when the Vietnamese would say on the loudspeaker, "Here is a new," if there was only one news item to report. Or, if there were several items to report, "Here are the news."

Within the group of prisoners, there were seven collaborators. "Seven more than were needed," says Thorsness. These were people who would cooperate with the enemy in order to get better food and treatment than the others—often at the others' expense.

Once this happened when the Vietnamese decided it would be nice to have certain prisoners read propaganda each day to the rest of the prisoners. The collaborators were happy to do this, even though they received direct orders from the ranking American prisoner not to.

Thorsness remembers, "We pleaded with them not to do it. We knew if they read, eventually the North Vietnamese would get tired of just the seven and decide it would be nice for everyone to read the propaganda. Finally, they would insist on it."

Thorsness was right. Eventually, the North Vietnamese started beating the rest of the prisoners who wouldn't read the stuff. It became another issue—an excuse for the mistreatment of prisoners.

When President Lyndon Johnson stopped the bombing in 1968, the prisoners thought they were going home soon. They figured it this way: "No commander in chief would ever give up the bombing, which was the best leverage we had, without getting us out. There had to be an agreement!" But later, when they heard that the peace negotiations in Geneva were concentrating on what shape the table should be, the prisoners became pretty disappointed. Days, months, and then years went by. Their commander in chief had sold them out.

After a while, the prisoners no longer allowed themselves to get emotional. When the peace accords were indeed signed, there was a provision that said the POWs should be told within five days. On the fifth morning, the Vietnamese camp commander called the prisoners out of their cells and announced that "no progress" had been made. Later that night, they had another announcement, and this time they were told the truth— that the agreements had been signed. "I don't understand how they benefited by lying to us earlier in the day," says Thorsness. "We still weren't sure whether to believe them."

The evidence became stronger when an international delegation, including some Americans, came to the prison. One of the Americans in the delegation whispered to Thorsness that he would be amazed by the treatment they were going to get when they got home.

Although the prisoners were now becoming convinced that their release might happen, there was still no celebration among them when the delegation left. They were too numb from years of suffering; they wouldn't allow themselves the vulnerability of hope.

But the time did come, after all. The men were separated into four groups as they left the prison. Thorsness was in the second group. He had been sick with malaria, but still he was put on a bus and taken to the flight line with the others. At the airstrip, hundreds of Vietnamese were watching the ceremony.

The prisoners stepped forward as each of their names were called. They walked up to the American C-141 airplane and were given over to an American air force colonel, whom they saluted. Two other American military personnel then escorted each man to the plane and gave him a beer. Inside the plane, the best-looking nurses in the Air Force were waiting. "No Navy women, just Air Force," insists Thorsness. But still there was no celebration, and no emotion was shown.

When the plane was closed up, some of the prisoners began to cry silently. Then the plane began to roll down the runway. After all the long years, the hope that they would soon be home was finally becoming real. When the airplane broke away from the ground, a tidal wave of emotion engulfed them. Everyone on the plane started to cry openly and celebrate. Thorsness remembers, "We were kissed and hugged by the nurses. And perhaps some of us may have even kissed back. We hugged each other. It was a wonderful two-hour flight. We were going home."

There were magazines and food on the plane. The prisoners could see from the magazines that the country's morality had changed. Thorsness felt disappointment about this. Americans also seemed less patriotic. Institutions were less trusted. Music was radically different. The prisoners saw pictures of kids wearing American flags on the seat of their pants.

America had changed. It was less confident in itself. Thorsness was coming back to his country more proud to be an American than when he left. It seemed the opposite had happened to the Americans at home.

When the prisoners stepped off the plane in the Philippines, many people were lined up to meet them. Thorsness looked over the crowd and commented to a friend, "Geez, they're fat!" Thorsness's own weight had gone from 175 to 115 pounds.

Thorsness called his wife from the Philippines and told her

he was coming home. When he landed in Hawaii, though, he was carried out of the plane in a litter. "I was so sick," he recalls. "They actually put me back in solitary confinement at the Tripler Army Hospital in Honolulu!" Thorsness again called his wife, who was waiting for him in Saint Louis. She said, "Okay, I'm coming over. I'll be there in twenty-four hours." But that wasn't necessary, as it turned out. For Thorsness, the Air Force loaded a doctor and some nurses into a C-141 for the flight home. It was strictly VIP treatment for the returning hero.

The plane took off that night and headed for Saint Louis. Thorsness asked the pilots to call him forward when San Francisco became visible on the early-morning horizon. Those lights had been the last thing he saw of America seven long years before. Later that night when he went into the cockpit and saw them again, the flight controllers in the San Francisco Control Area started playing the song "Don't Fence Me In" over the radio. "Welcome home, Homecoming 7," they said. "We advise, you have presidential clearance from your present position direct to Saint Louis. Good luck, sir." And for a farm kid from Walnut Grove, Minnesota, that wasn't bad.

Thorsness remembers, "When I landed, I saw my beautiful eleven-year-old daughter who had somehow turned eighteen, and I saw my beautiful wife once again."

Thinking back, Thorsness says, "It's nice to be singled out to receive the Medal of Honor. But I wear my Honor humbly because I know there were better and stronger men than me in that prison; men like Robby Reisner from Oklahoma, Jim Stockdale—even though he was just a Navy guy—and Jack Roamer, whom I lived with, prayed with, and went to torture with. These men are my heroes."

Nowadays we often hear that heroes are missing from our modern society. And it's true that John Wayne, Will Rogers, and Babe Ruth are gone. But a deeper truth may be that there are lesser known men who deserve the title more, and are still with us—men like Medal of Honor recipient Leo K. Thorsness.

2.

PATRICK HENRY BRADY

Thank You, Double Nickel

Medals of Honor awarded to men during combat are often for actions in which enemy soldiers are killed or important pieces of land are taken or held. Bravery, however, can also be responsible for saving lives.

Major Patrick Brady, a legend among Vietnam helicopter rescue pilots, often risked his life to save lives. In fact, during two tours of duty in Vietnam, helicopters piloted by Brady rescued more than five thousand men from battlefields, often when the landing zone was under fire and no one else would go in.

Patrick Henry Brady
Major, U.S. Army
Near Chu Lai, Republic of Vietnam
6 January 1968

The Vietnam War was mostly fought by infantry and helicopters. To the infantry troops, the words *Dust Off* represented security: men in helicopters who would go into almost any situation and rescue them when they were wounded.

The Dust Off crews flew the medical evacuation (medevac) Huey helicopters. These crews had one of the most dangerous jobs in the war. They were shot down three times more often than any other aviators, and lives often depended on their success when they were called into hot landing zones. Many Dust Off crews died trying to save lives.

One of the legendary Dust Off pilots was Major Patrick Brady, also known as "Double Nickel." Patrick Brady projects a striking presence today, and most surely must have done so then. Handsome and self-assured, with an attitude that does not very easily suffer the company of fools, Brady does the job put before him.

Raised in a sometimes unstable home environment, he found himself and acceptance from others by playing sports at the strict O'Dea High School in Seattle, Washington. He still has a numbness in his fingers from the frequent slaps with a leather strap that he received from the Catholic brothers who ran the school.

During college at Seattle University, Brady figured it was inevitable he would be drafted. He had been told that an officer could sleep in his own room while a draftee slept in a barracks full of men; and so, Patrick Brady decided to get serious about the ROTC. Indeed, upon graduation, he entered the Army as an officer.

After flight school in 1964, Brady went to Vietnam for his first tour of duty. He became a medevac helicopter pilot and started learning the business of rescuing people from battle-

fields. "Our helicopters were beautiful machines," Brady recalls. "Those Bell UH-1 Hueys were 'state of the art' Cadillacs.
They were powerful, powerful things."

The early Dust Off pilots were the first people in Vietnam to
fly at night, and they were the first people to land on the bat-
tlefield while the troops were still under fire. Brady started
developing technical flying skills that most aviators just didn't
have. In fact, many people thought Brady and the other early
Dust Offs had received special training for their jobs. They
hadn't. They just wanted to get those patients out of there, and
they were willing to fly at night and into hot battlefields to do
so. "I couldn't imagine leaving a landing zone without the pa-
tient, no matter what was going on," says Brady.

Each helicopter had a medic and a crew chief in the backseats.
Some of the choppers had two side-mounted M-16 guns. When
Brady was still learning his business, he let the men on the
ground give him a "bad minute" before landing. This was a
time when fire was purposely created in all directions immediately preceding the helicopter's landing in the zone.

"The guys on the ground thought this would protect us,"
remembers Brady. "But then my guys in the door of the helicopter would shoot too, and the next thing you heard were
bullets everywhere. Pretty soon, you couldn't tell if the bullets
were incoming or outgoing fire." Finally, Brady insisted he
wanted it quiet when he came in so he could tell what was
really going on.

As Brady was learning his business in 1964, he started realizing other things too. When a Dust Off was called, the guys
on the ground usually needed it badly and they wouldn't always
be very objective when describing their landing zone security.
After experiencing a few unpleasant surprises, Brady concluded
that, if he was being called into a landing zone, that area—by
definition—was not secure. So he started just asking the soldiers
on the ground whether they would be willing to stand in the
landing zone and help load the patients. If they were, he would
come—simple as that.

As Brady approached a landing zone, he would ask the guys

on the ground where the last enemy contact had occurred and what kind of weapons they had. "Once I had this information, I would form a picture in my mind of the terrain and the landing zone," explains Brady. "Then, I would try to put my eyeballs in the enemy's head and imagine what he could see. If I was using my imagination right, a kind of highway would spring up from the area which would take me right from the sky into the landing area. This landing would then be as safe as anything could be."

This technique must have worked because Brady and the few other early Dust Offs covered all of South Vietnam, developing landing and extraction techniques that eventually saved many lives. Men who would otherwise have died were lifted from battlefields and brought to hospitals, and they lived.

"Our helicopters had trained medics, trained pilots, and aircraft that had the medical equipment needed to keep a soldier alive until we could get him to the hospital," says Brady. "This worked. If a soldier was shot in a rice paddy in Vietnam, he had a better chance of survival than if he were in a crash on a highway in America. If we could get our hands on a guy still alive, he was probably going to live. We had great surgical talent over there and plenty of blood."

During one mission in March 1964, a lot of guys were in a great deal of trouble. Brady began carrying patients out of an area as fast as he could. During a refueling stop in the middle of the battle, Brady was approached and asked if he would take ammunition back to people on the ground with his next trip in. Evidently, American soldiers were surrounded and they were running out of ammunition. Brady had the only helicopter available; but according to the Geneva Convention, medevac helicopters could not be used to move ammunition.

Brady replied, "Sure, I'll help you." His copilot was apprehensive. He had been in country longer than Brady, and he didn't think it was right to do what they were planning. Brady told him, "I can't leave these guys without ammunition." They brought the ammo in.

Later that day, a spotter plane was shot down. Brady flew

into the jungle and landed near the crash sight and found both pilots dead. Again in violation of Geneva Conventions' rules, which prohibit the transport of dead people in medevac helicopters, Brady ordered the bodies placed in the helicopter and he flew them back to base. Brady wasn't sure whether his commander was going to understand these rule violations.

"That night we got back to base well after midnight," Brady remembers. Major Charles Kelley, the commander, was waiting to have a few words with him. "Brady, what were you thinking when you took those dead guys out?" Apparently, the story had gotten around. Brady told his commander, "I'll never leave an area with dead soldiers on the ground if I can help it." Major Kelley stared at Brady and asked, "What about taking that ammunition in?" This time Brady looked closely at his commander and said, "I was practicing preventive medicine." Kelley started to smile, and then both men broke into a laugh. And that was that. From then on, Brady took bodies out of battle zones and, if necessary, he brought ammunition to soldiers when they needed it. Nobody bothered him about it again.

In 1964, there was only one medevac helicopter unit in Vietnam. Five helicopters were covering the entire country. Brady and his unit carried more than four thousand patients, working ten straight months without a day off. This was intense training, but the Dust Off business was being learned.

When Brady returned to Vietnam for his second tour in 1967, there were two hundred Dust Off aircraft in Vietnam. He was now a thirty-three-year-old major who was second in command of the 54th, his own forty-man Dust Off unit. And Brady was looking forward to getting back to business.

"They gave us six brand-new Hueys, H models," Brady remembers. "Our pilots were new too; they all graduated from flight school on the same day in June 1967. I think they thought they were handpicked to be Dust Offs, but they must have gotten suspicious when they realized every one of their names started with an 'S.' The only thing these guys knew was what I taught them! I'll tell you right now, they were a piece of work." The 54th had only three people with any experience at all, and everyone was young. But they wanted to do well.

When the men first arrived in Vietnam, the unit didn't even have a place to go. Brady scouted around until he found a place to set up their base at Chu Lai. "You would think this would be planned out," says Brady. "It wasn't. I found an open airfield and we brought the unit in." Later the aircraft came.

The new pilots were eager to learn, and Brady taught them the fundamentals of tactical flying. He also helped them understand night and bad-weather flying. Brady was the most experienced flyer around, out of everyone in the unit and the operations officer as well. The experience from his previous tour was invaluable.

Brady was surprised by the amount of construction talent in the unit. There were tradesmen like carpenters, mechanics, and electricians. This gave Brady an idea.

The officer controlling commodities and materials in Chu Lai was a Colonel Brady. So, Patrick Brady started going around to people and bragging that his "uncle," Colonel Brady, would want him to have this lumber, or this cement, or those nails. "This technique helped us get the things we wanted, and we wanted a lot," Brady remembers. Pretty soon, Brady's new unit had enough material to start building their own facilities. And the facilities they built...

"We staked out a square in the rear area of the air base and built enough hootches so everyone in the unit had his own room," Brady recalls. "We built an operations shack with a bunker behind it which also served as our bar, between mortar attacks. On the other end of our claimed area, we put up a rock-faced, two-story building which had sauna baths, another bar, and a five-thousand-volume library! That one took a little negotiation."

With only forty men in the 54th, Brady actually had to do a lot of "scrounging" to get all this material. But because he had been in Vietnam before, he was actually quite good at this. Between this talent and his "uncle," the compound's construction went along quite nicely. There were cement walkways and running water. In the middle of the compound, the men built a pond surrounded with tiki lights. "These guys were talented," remembers Brady. The compound even had bicycles.

"On my first tour we had a pet python, some myna birds, and a pet ocelot," remembers Brady. "We loved our animals. So on this second tour, I went out to get the men a pig." Yes, a pig. Brady went to a local bar and found a Vietnamese woman who liked his wristwatch. Unfortunately, she didn't have a pig to trade for it. But she did have a goose. Later that day, Brady was back on base with the unit's new pet: a goose who was immediately dubbed "our feathered pig," Gertrude. It wasn't long, however, until the unit got a pig too, whom they named Superoink. Both of these animals got along quite well with the unit's new monkey named Frances, and its dog named Dusty.

"Superoink grew up with our dog Dusty," recalls Brady. "He thought he was a dog, too. The pig played with the dog, slept with the dog, and acted like a dog. Gertrude, our goose, was another story; she was very mean. She would constantly chase Frances, our monkey, and bite her. Frances would run away by diving into the pond to swim with the other geese. The guys just loved Frances. Most monkeys are mean and ugly, but Frances was beautiful."

Once, Frances fell off a bicycle and cracked her head open. The men felt terrible. Brady found a neurosurgeon who was willing to x-ray Frances's head and bandage her up. "She developed a limp after this and she stopped swimming," remembers Brady. "But the guys were glad she was still alive."

And for vacations . . . Brady found a small island along the coast of Chu Lai, about twenty minutes flying time from the base. There was an old Japanese grass airstrip there and it was a gorgeous place. The island's only inhabitant was a Navy lieutenant manning a radar site. Brady made arrangements for his men to come to the island for R&R. "This was an absolutely safe and secure island," Brady recalls. "If the guys got spooky about getting shot or killed, I would fly them out to the island for three or four days' rest. In our kind of constant combat, the guys had to be watched closely for fatigue."

The unit's beautiful living area, and their pets, did help to keep the men relaxed. Their regular barbecues, the availability of running water, and even a big freezer for food, were all ways of keeping Brady's men from thinking about getting shot at each day. "A guy will get nervous and apprehensive after a while and it's hard to deal with him unless you give him a break," says Brady. "He becomes ineffective and then dangerous."

The men worked hard—sometimes as long as twenty-four straight hours. Often they would have missions seven days a week, for weeks at a time. "Flying like this, it was important to have a good environment for the men to live in," says Brady. "That's what I made sure they had."

The weather in the Mekong Delta was often bad, but bad weather didn't stop the pilots. When the weather wasn't a problem, other conditions were. The men dealt with confined jungle areas, mountain pinnacles, fires, and combat on a daily basis. They knew all too well that their work was dangerous.

One night in October 1967, Brady was needed in a place called "Death Valley." When he got there, he found mountains and a valley completely covered with clouds. Someone on the mountainside "popped" a flare; in the momentary flash, Brady could see the silhouette of the mountain—which allowed him to come down and make the pickup. This experience stuck in Brady's mind because it was always a problem getting in to pick up people on night-weather missions in the mountains. This flair "technique" worked for him.

Later the same month Brady got another weather call. It was night and he had a "float ship," which was used when the regular aircraft were down. About twenty people needed evacuation from a valley in which a tropical storm was raging. Seventy-nautical-mile-an-hour winds were blowing and there was no ceiling. Going into the area, Brady ran into an inkwell of rain and clouds. He was near a mountain but he could see nothing.

First he turned on his landing lights and tried to follow trails. But the light would only reflect off the rain, making it even harder to see. Next he tried to come around a river. Again, he couldn't do it. Then he remembered the mountain and the flare from the earlier mission.

Brady asked the ground troops to start shooting flares straight up into the rain. Brady went down to seven thousand feet and began following the flares down through the dense rain and clouds. He made four trips that night, using this technique, and got everyone out. It had never been done before. For Brady, the problem of night-weather missions had been solved: the solution was to use flares, along with a liberal sprinkling of flying skill, daring, and luck.

Dust Offs also had to deal with low valley fog on daytime missions. Often, mountain peaks could be seen poking out of a fog of "solid soup" down to a few hundred feet. Since getting under the fog could get you to your destination, the trick was to get underneath without running into the ground or a mountain.

One afternoon, Brady got a call for help. A soldier with a snakebite was on the side of a mountain, and afternoon clouds had socked him in. When Brady got to the mountain, it was completely blanketed with clouds.

First he flew to a clear area in the valley, got under the clouds, and started up the mountainside. "I got into some thick stuff," remembers Brady. "I figured if things got bad, I could fall back into the valley." Things did get bad. Starting up the mountain into the clouds, Brady lost all visibility. This was pretty dangerous, so he fell back into the valley and broke below the clouds.

Just as he did, one of the soldiers on the mountain started screaming into the radio that the snakebitten soldier was going into convulsions. "I knew I needed to get in there, but I didn't know how to do it," remembers Brady. "I came around again and the wind hit us. It hit us so hard, we were thrown sideways. My side window was open and I looked out thinking we were going to crash." Regaining control, Brady sighted his rotor tip and a treetop. With these two reference points, he knew he was right side up.

This was all he needed. "I turned that sucker sideways and started up the mountain again," remembers Brady. "This time my head was out the window watching my rotor tips and the tops of the trees as we flew sideways up the mountain."

Brady made it to the soldier and took him to the hospital. And that's the way it was done from then on. For Brady, the problem of daylight heavy-fog missions had now been solved, as well. Again, flying skill, daring, and a lot of confidence were all essential.

Because of his developing weather-flying skill, anytime there was a bad-weather mission Brady was called. He was the most experienced Dust Off pilot and he knew how to fly the "flare missions." Now he was developing his "rotor tip/treetop" technique.

Strictly speaking, Brady was not even on duty the day of his Medal of Honor missions. There was "first up" and "second up." But because he was the unit's operations officer, he was always on duty.

Brady was awakened just before daybreak. There were some wounded Vietnamese needing evacuation from an outpost. "They called me because this was a 'flare mission' and other crews couldn't get in," Brady recalls. "We got in there and found a very thick, low, valley fog." Moving to the side and then underneath the clouds, Brady followed trails into the area.

Quickly loading the Vietnamese wounded onto the helicopter, Brady made his way to a hospital. Later he was told his helicopter had been under fire during the mission; but because he saw so little, he didn't even know it. A ground eyewitness reported that the helicopter had been shelled by mortar fire. But again, as far as Brady was concerned, there was nothing out of the ordinary on this first mission of what was to be a pretty interesting day.

Brady had just got back to base when he received another

call. This time, two helicopters had crashed while trying to get to sixty patients trapped in another valley under fog. Nobody could get in. And this time, patients were dying. Brady immediately contacted the brigade commander at a fire support base overlooking the valley, and asked for the radio frequency of the men on the ground. The brigade commander refused to give it, saying he didn't want any more helicopters crashing in the valley. Brady immediately flew to the fire support base.

"It was still early morning and the command base was on the top of a mountain," Brady remembers. "Down in the valley, where the wounded troops were, there was a fog cover extending up six hundred feet." The fire support base was firing artillery off the high ground into the valley.

The commander insisted he didn't want more helicopters to go into the valley, and he especially didn't want to lift his artillery fire. "I knew how to get in there," Brady remembers. "In fact, I didn't think there would be a problem, as long as I had the ground frequency. But the commander wouldn't give it to me. I didn't even want him to stop his artillery fire!"

Finally, the brigade commander took Brady's copilot aside and said, "Can he really get in there?" The copilot looked straight at the commander, paused, and simply said, "Yes, sir." The commander approached Brady and asked him the same thing. Brady replied that he could, if he had the ground frequency. The commander told Brady he wouldn't lift the artillery fire. Brady said that was fine. The brigade commander then figured that, if this guy was willing to still go in under these circumstances, he deserved a shot. Brady got his frequency.

"The ground troops weren't that far away," Brady remembers. "But I couldn't go straight down through the stuff. Instead, I flew to a clear area on the side and tried to get under the fog to find a trail in." Four other helicopters started in with Brady so that all the patients could be pulled out at the same time.

Soon the four following aircraft aborted because the fog was too thick. This was actually a relief to Brady because, in stuff this heavy, it wasn't safe with the other helicopters around.

Brady kept his head out the window and, flying sideways, kept his rotor tips lined with the treetops. Keeping a slight forward angle to blow fog away with the blade backwash, he moved through zero visibility toward the troops. This was incredible helicopter flying.

"The first time in, I dropped off a medical team to sort out the patients," Brady remembers. "I went in four more times to get all the patients; and each time, I did an instrument take off straight up through the fog." Every time Brady returned, he was flying directly over North Vietnamese troops who fired directly into his helicopter.

American soldiers at the mountain firebase could see Brady's helicopter repeatedly pop up from the fog on the valley floor, and each time they would start cheering. They knew what was going on. When the patients had all been evacuated and Brady returned to the firebase strip, everyone was standing at attention, including the brigade commander. They were saluting.

"The whole countryside was alive that day," Brady remembers. "We got another hot mission, this time to the Melei area." The helicopter started toward a landing zone and began taking heavy ground fire. The aircraft was hit several times. Brady checked his instruments. The helicopter was still flying, so he continued into the hot landing zone. After loading the patients, he flew to the hospital. There the crew got a new helicopter, just as they heard that another Dust Off bird was working in a minefield.

The minefield was close, so Brady headed that way. Over the radio, he heard that a mine had gone off. People were killed right next to the Dust Off, and the pilot had lifted out. Brady was just arriving. The people on the ground started screaming on the radio for help. "Dust Off, Dust Off, come back, we have seriously wounded here."

"I saw where the other helicopter had been sitting," remembers Brady. "I knew if I landed where he had been, I would be pretty safe. I thought I would be, anyway." Brady watched the skid marks from the previous helicopter and put his bird down there. He hoped his rotor blades wouldn't set off a mine. Luckily, they didn't.

Brady could see wounded lying all around. "Then, talk about courage," remembers Brady. "My crew jumped out of our bird and into the minefield! They started carrying patients back."

Brady and his copilot were sitting by their controls waiting for the wounded to be loaded. Then suddenly, a mine went off. "I was watching my crew chief and medic carry a litter with someone on it and they were blown into the air," Brady recalls. "I think they had a dead person on the litter already. His leg was already bent behind his neck and the blast blew it off. The body took most of the blast and this saved my crew. But a good part of the explosion blew into the aircraft, too."

By now, seven or eight men were already loaded on the helicopter, and Brady's crew dived back in. When the helicopter took off, all the warning lights came on. "We didn't know if the thing would keep flying: my panel was lit right up," remembers Brady. "I had dying people on that aircraft and I knew we had to get them to a hospital." Staying close to the ground on the principle that he wouldn't have as far to fall, Brady struggled to fly his helicopter back to the hospital. His crew survived, but again his helicopter didn't.

Taking off in his third helicopter of the day, and with different crews, Brady continued flying missions and bringing people in. "This was a pretty full day," admits Brady. "We brought in over a hundred people."

"I get a high from saving lives," he says. "You don't think about the danger as much as you think about helping men who need you. In Vietnam, I was faced with a series of obstacles: enemy fire, terrain, or aircraft limitations. I worked my way through those obstacles and brought human beings to safety. This was a thrill. It was what I needed to do and it was also my job."

Brady's 54th may have been one of the most effective combat units ever. In the ten months Brady was with the unit, more than ten thousand patients were evacuated from battlefields to hospitals—more than were evacuated by helicopter during the entire Korean War. "We averaged 117 percent of our aircraft damaged by enemy fire each month," says Brady. "Seven of our six assigned helicopters were shot each month. And at any time, we only averaged three usable aircraft." In the 54th's forty-man detachment, there were twenty-three Purple Hearts given, along with more than forty Distinguished Service Crosses, Silver Stars, Bronze Stars, and Distinguished Flying Crosses. Brady's unit was not only one of the most appreciated outfits in the war, but it may have been one of the most highly decorated ever.

On October 9, 1969, President Richard Nixon presented to Patrick Henry Brady the country's highest military honor: the Congressional Medal of Honor. This, along with his Distinguished Service Cross and four Distinguished Flying Crosses, is meant to show this hero that his country is proud of him, and that more than five thousand soldiers and their families are still grateful to him for risking his life for them, above and beyond the call of duty.

Thank you, Double Nickel.

Part II

LAND

3.

JIMMIE E. HOWARD

The Team Player

In any sport, the characteristic of tenacity, of never giving
up, is not only an honorable tradition; sometimes, it wins
the game. In 1966, a team of a different sort was on a hill
in Vietnam, and they were losing. The odds were firmly
against them, but they stuck with it because their team
captain wouldn't give up. These men—every one of them
wounded and with only eight bullets left between them—
eventually rallied to produce one of the greatest come-
backs in history. Tenacity, comradeship, and teamwork—
these are also characteristics of Medal of Honor recipients.

Jimmie E. Howard
Staff Sergeant, U.S. Marine Corps
Republic of Vietnam
16 June 1966

Born in Burlington, Iowa, on July 27, 1929, Jimmie Howard grew up excelling in track and football. He even went to the University of Iowa on a football scholarship. In July 1950 when the Korean War broke out, though, Howard joined the Marines. "I was full of piss and vinegar and I just wanted to do good," he says.

Howard went overseas and fought in Korea for seventeen months. While there, he was wounded three times and received three Purple Hearts and a Silver Star. By the end of the war, he was a Marine corporal. "Korea taught me to keep my eyes open," Howard remembers. "It taught me self-preservation and how to look out for the enemy. My experiences there made me a smarter Marine."

By the time Howard got to Vietnam thirteen years later, he was a well-trained combat veteran and the war was in full gear. Howard was a platoon sergeant in Charlie Company, 1st Reconnaissance Battalion, of the famed 1st Marine Division. His unit conducted long-range reconnaissance patrols.

Howard had been in country for six months when his Medal of Honor patrol occurred. The Marine mission was to establish a position on Hill 488, a barren rocky elevation overlooking the Hiep Duc Valley about twenty miles northwest of Chu Lai. Their orders were to call in air and artillery strikes on the enemy in this area. A North Vietnamese regimental headquarters was supposed to be nearby, and there were enemy soldiers everywhere.

Howard's eighteen-man platoon dropped by helicopter into the operation area. From the valley surrounded by high hills, the platoon quietly made its way to the top of Hill 488. The Marines dug in at sunset of the first night. They hadn't been seen by the enemy.

Howard's hilltop observation site was about five miles from

the ocean. His position overlooked the valley floor from a fifteen-hundred-foot elevation. At the top of the hill, it was no more than twenty-five yards across, with only a single large boulder for cover. But Howard believed that, if problems occurred, his men would have a possible escape route to the ocean on the east.

He set up three teams on the finger ridges descending from the top of the hill. Each team of five men was about fifty yards from the center, and each Marine had instructions to withdraw immediately to the top in the event of enemy contact. The platoon "headquarters" was there at the hill's small and exposed flat top. Howard and the platoon corpsman positioned themselves there, along with the radio that later saved their lives.

That night, Howard and his men could see many lights in the valley below them. The lights appeared and then disappeared. These were lanterns carried by the North Vietnamese troops making their way on the trails across the valley floor. Howard was hoping the North Vietnamese didn't know his Marines were on the hill. They waited throughout the night, and nothing happened.

The first full day on the hill saw excellent success for their mission, as Howard and his men called in artillery and air attacks on enemy concentrations. Secondary explosions were heard and lots of fire was seen in the valley below. The enemy was being hit hard. It seemed worthwhile to stay put.

During the second night on the hill, the lights from the night before appeared to be getting closer. But again, nothing more happened.

The next day on the hill proved to be another success: more firepower was directed on the enemy. Huge columns of smoke were seen rising from the valley floor after artillery and bombs were directed in. Howard's men plotted the air and artillery strikes with such success that finally their commander, Lieutenant Colonel Arthur Sullivan—located at Loc San about three miles to the northwest—ordered no more strikes on enemy positions unless a spotter aircraft could be seen working the area. The commander hoped the enemy would think the accurate firing information was coming from the spotter aircraft rather than from this well-positioned hill platoon.

"I thought one more night on the hill wouldn't hurt us," remembers Howard. "I didn't realize the enemy already knew we were there and I also didn't realize we were already surrounded. I did know we would be alone, and on our own, if problems occurred on Hill 488 that night."

During the night of June 15, 1966, Corporal Ricardo Binns was sitting at his position on the tip of one of the finger ridges fifty yards from the top of the hill. He remembers, "I thought I saw something move and I fired. A guy screamed from the bushes and all hell broke out."

The Marine teams immediately withdrew to their center command post. The roar of fire and the flashes of enemy muzzles surrounded the Marines. Enemy soldiers began spilling into the Marine central position. Hand-to-hand combat began.

"I radioed to Colonel Sullivan that we needed help," Howard remembers. The Marine's planned escape route was filled with enemy soldiers. The colonel immediately understood the desperate situation and requested Air Force and Marine air support for the surrounded Marines.

The first combat aircraft raced in, but they couldn't see anything on this moonless night. So they waited. Finally, the C-47 flare aircraft arrived. When the first flare opened up, Howard could hear one of his Marines exclaim, "Look at them all! It's like ants on an anthill!"

The Air Force and Marine jets from Da Nang and Chu Lai began their deadly duty. "They bombed and strafed the hell out of the enemy," Howard remembers. "I think they cut the attackers off from any reinforcements. Now we just had to handle the enemy soldiers already on the hill."

The jets made their runs and the helicopters immediately followed, firing their guns at the hillside. This went on and on as the enemy attackers drove closer to the surrounded Marines.

Throughout the night, Howard went from Marine to Marine, shouting encouragement and firing his rifle from the hottest positions. The Marines continuously improved their fields of fire and rained a killing shower of destruction on the attackers. But the intensity of the attack didn't let up. Howard would periodically return to the radio and report the situation to Colonel Sullivan: "Six, this is Carnival Time. I need more support. My kids can't take this much longer. If we can't get more help, we aren't going to be here by morning." Other times he would simply tell his commander, "Please tell my wife and kids I love them."

Lieutenant Colonel Sullivan had personally taken charge of the radio on the other end, and was calling in the air strikes. He kept telling Howard, "Tiger, hang in there. I'll get you relief. I'll get it for you." Sullivan's involvement was so intense that, by the end of the night, he was almost brought up for court-martial because of his aggressiveness with superiors, trying to raise adequate air support for Howard and his platoon.

"I didn't think we were going to get out of there," Howard remembers.

Throughout the night, the open firefight on the hill continued. Intermittent hand-to-hand combat occurred when enemy soldiers broke through. The Marines were completely surrounded, and 450 enemy attackers continued a relentless advance into the M-14 fire of the desperate American Marines. The fighting was so intense that at times the enemy line held only ten feet from the small American position.

Gunfire and the explosion of hand grenades were everywhere. Mortar shells, with shrapnel pieces, were flying freely. Corporal Jerrald Thompson was killed by an enemy K-bar knife. He was found the next morning with his hand on a knife handle embedded in an enemy's abdomen, while an enemy knife was embedded in Thompson's back. Lance Corporal John Adams emptied his gun into the advancing enemy and then, severely wounded, he struggled to his feet and fell into a group of attackers. He killed three more with the butt and bayonet of his empty gun before he was finally killed.

Each wave of attackers was repulsed, but blood flowed freely on the hill. Fifty-caliber machine gun fire from the enemy was answered with intensity and spirit by the surrounded Marines. American cries of "I'm hit!" were coming from all sides.

Halfway through the night, a mortar shell exploded near Howard, and shrapnel hit him in the leg and groin. Howard was losing a lot of blood until Corpsman Billie Holmes was finally able to stop it with a big "diaper bandage." The pain made it difficult for Howard to move around. When the corpsman offered him morphine for the pain, though, Howard refused, saying, "Now is not the time for me to get dopey."

The intense fighting continued. The North Vietnamese realized that no reinforcements for the Marines could get in there that night, and they also knew that the air fire would not hurt them as long as they stayed directly on the Marine's position. The Marines were outnumbered twenty to one, but they fought the enemy to a standstill. Howard started shouting to his men, "Keep it up, you gyrenes! We're going to make it out of here."

The shrill enemy combat whistles continued blowing, and the loud clacking of the attackers' bamboo sticks produced a sound that was weird to the surviving Marines. But the violent screams of the attackers were met again and again by desperate fire from the Marines. Wounded men too injured to fight began cheering on their comrades. Some would warn the others when grenades fell nearby; others would try to resupply ammunition. Death and bravery showed itself in both the attacked and the attackers.

The jets kept up their fire under the light of the continuous flares from the C-47 airplanes. F-105 Thuds swept in and tore into the enemy. Marine Crusaders scorched the sides of the hill, toasting the faces of the Marines with their weapons' deadly heat. They actually laid their fire inside the first circles described by their fire-zone instruments. Sometimes they would come in and "wave off" because they were just too close to the Marines. The bombs, rockets, and strafing had never been laid down so close to American soldiers. The Vietnamese started to burrow into the hill to escape the hellish air fire.

Finally there was a lull in the attack. Then the North Vietnamese started chanting in their singsong English, "Marine, you going to die in a hour. It's all over for you. You will die, Marine." A thought suddenly occurred to Howard, and he said to his men, "Let's give them the old horse laugh on the count of three."

Seldom in the annals of military history has anything more incredible happened. This small handful of wounded, outnumbered, and surrounded Marines—with no hope for reinforcements until morning—started laughing. They laughed at their attackers, they laughed at their danger, and they laughed at their death. They laughed as loud as they could for several minutes. Then there was complete silence on both sides.

You could have heard a pin drop.

The effect of this display of mockery was so genuine that enemy soldiers, captured later in the war, admitted that their confidence had been shattered. "How could these Marines laugh at us? What did they know that we didn't?"

And after that, the fighting spirit of the enemy changed.

Just before dawn, Howard yelled to his men, "Reveille! Reveille! It's time to get up." This ridiculous statement was followed by laughter from his men again. The enemy could hear these crazy Marines, and they didn't understand.

After a night of almost continuous fighting, Howard's men were getting low on bullets and hand grenades. Howard ordered them to start throwing rocks. He had learned the trick in Korea: if the enemy thought a hand grenade had been thrown, they might move and be seen; then the Marines could shoot them. It worked. In fact, it worked several times.

By now, the Marines realized they were about to receive the final push from their Vietnamese attackers. It was almost daylight, and the enemy knew they had only one more chance.

With their ammunition nearly gone, the Marines figured their final fight to the death was about to begin.

So, one Marine pulled out his ten-inch K-bar knife and jammed it into the ground beside him. He was ready for his final stand. K-bar knives started coming out all around the Marine perimeter, and were being angrily jammed into the ground. The men were ready for the last stand even though, by now, everyone had been wounded. And there were only eight bullets left in the entire platoon!

Then a faint chop was heard in the distance. At first it was hard to hear, but eventually it became the overwhelming roar of twenty-seven American helicopters. In the early morning sky over in the direction of Chu Lai could be seen the welcome sight of transports carrying the 250 men from Charlie Company of the 5th Marines. The besieged platoon watched as their life-saving replacements dropped below them to the southwest. These fresh Marines immediately started tearing their way up the hill through the now retreating enemy soldiers, coming to the rescue of the Marine platoon. The final enemy attack never happened.

Howard's Marines had held and survived.

Billie Holmes, the platoon medic, was still moving around taking care of his wounded troops. When the medivac helicopters came in, the remaining men of the platoon were loaded on board. Only twelve wounded Marines were left from the original eighteen, and Howard refused to leave the area until every one of his men was accounted for. Only when Corpsman Holmes came up to him and said, "Top Notch, we have all men accounted for," did Howard finally get onto the helicopter and return to base for medical care along with his men.

In addition to the Purple Hearts given to every man in Howard's platoon, thirteen men received the Silver Star, four received the Navy Cross, and Jimmie Howard received the Medal of Honor. This unit became the most decorated platoon in the two hundred years of U.S. military history.

On August 21, 1967, President Lyndon Johnson presented to Jimmie Howard his Congressional Medal of Honor. Attending the ceremony was Lieutenant Colonel Arthur Sullivan, the commander who had taken such an aggressive role calling in support for Howard's platoon that night. Also present were the eleven surviving members of the heroic platoon.

During the ceremony, when President Johnson asked Howard if he would like to say something into the microphone, the Marine looked at the president and then pointed to his troops in the audience and said, "Sir, those are the men that did it." He then touched the president's arm and led him to the men of his platoon and introduced every one of them.

Later, as Howard was walking to the Red Room in the White House, a Marine lieutenant colonel who was on the president's staff grabbed Howard's arm and told him he had just embarrassed the U.S. Marine Corps. Howard asked how. "Because, the president does not meet people like that," the lieutenant colonel replied, referring to Howard's men.

Howard was walking with his wife, General Lewis Walt, and General Ray Davis, the commandant of the Marine Corps. When General Walt heard this criticism from the lieutenant colonel, he said, "The gunny did it his way." Then the general asked the lieutenant colonel to report to him the next morning. Three days later, the officer was reassigned from his prestigious White House job to duty in Vietnam, where he could learn a different perspective on respect and honor.

"The Team" has always been important to Jimmie Howard. From his high school football days in Iowa to the top of Hill 488, it was The Team he played for. And it was on behalf of his men—believing them to be the heroes of that night so long ago—that Jimmie Howard received then, and carries out now, the responsibilities of Medal of Honor recipient.

4.

MATT URBAN

Walk Tall and Hold Your Head High

The Medal of Honor is sometimes awarded to men who show incredible persistence. This persistence may be demonstrated as a continuous pursuit of duty, or maybe even just an inability to take no for an answer.

Matt Urban wouldn't accept being told he couldn't join his men for the North African invasion. And twice, after severe wounds in France, he wouldn't accept doctors' telling him he couldn't go back with his men in combat. During two-and-a-half critical months of World War II's European invasion, Matt Urban showed his men inspiring combat leadership as well as a single-minded pursuit of the enemy. This was a man who fought the war to win.

Matt Urban is a competitor. Born in Buffalo, New York, on August 29, 1919, Urban was never one to turn his back on a challenge. He went through school excelling in sports. In fact, at Cornell University—where boxing was his love—he became university champion in three different weight classes! When he graduated from college in June 1941, another fight was waiting for him—this one not so near home.

"The winds of war were blowing pretty hard then, so I decided to join the Army," remembers Urban. "Immediately, I loved the military." Urban entered the Army as a lieutenant, and his first assignment was as the recreation officer at Fort Bragg, North Carolina. He trained there until it was time to ship out for the invasion of North Africa.

Because of a special assignment as the 60th Infantry's boxing coaches, both Urban and a Sergeant Sebock missed shipping out with their regular unit. They ended up on another ship named the *Florence Nightingale*. "My ship to Africa was a ship of outcasts," remembers Urban. "You'd think a ship with a name like that would not be a fighting man's ship, and it wasn't."

By the time his ship anchored in North Africa, the other troops in the convoy were already preparing for a combat landing. Sergeant Sebock and Lieutenant Urban went to the colonel who was in charge of the troops and asked for permission to reunite with their own company for the beach landing. The colonel refused their request and told Urban he was "being saved for recreation assignments." This wasn't what Urban wanted to hear. Because he already suspected that his recreation officer duties were holding him back from the combat assignments he wanted, he decided to go on this beach landing anyway.

"Sergeant Sebock and I jumped ship," remembers Urban. "We left the ship on a little rubber raft and started to shore. I remember the colonel yelling at us from the deck to come back."

Men were already landing on the beach. Approaching the shore, Urban and Sebock realized that men were drowning around them, everywhere. The Army had given the men packs that were too heavy. Urban and the sergeant started pulling men out of the water, and kept pulling them out until they had dragged about a dozen men into shore.

Later that day, Urban was able to rejoin his own company in the 2nd Battalion, 60th Infantry Regiment of the 9th Infantry Division. As Urban tells it, "Our men were being shot up and killed fairly regularly. During that first day of battle, we lost three sergeants." This was the men's first experience with combat, and they fought hard. "We paid the price for not being more experienced," remembers Urban. "During the next three days, we finally secured the airfield, which was our objective."

Urban and his men were now veterans. There was no more waiting, no more thinking about what combat was really like, no more wondering about what they would do when the guns started firing. They now knew what battle was, and they knew how they would react. They also knew they could do it. "Going over, we had boyhood visions that war was like cops and robbers," says Urban. "But wow, when we hit that shore, we woke up pretty quick."

It was November 1942, and the Americans were going after Germany's Field Marshal Erwin Rommel with a vengeance. "We went throughout Africa after that man," Urban recalls. "We were on foot, and for three months we fought him."

During one battle, Urban's Fox Company was assigned to capture a hill that the British hadn't been able to take for sixty days. The men concealed themselves and then outmaneuvered the Germans during their attack, and ended up taking the hill. Matt Urban remembers, "For three days, we were surrounded. Our company continued to hold this hill despite counterattacks by German regiment-sized forces. Finally, they gave up and withdrew to Bizerte."

Bizerte, Africa, became the last point of German resistance. The men of Urban's company were the first foot soldiers into this town. And so ended Rommel's African campaign and Urban's first sustained combat.

"We became a war machine," recalls Urban. "My men were combat veterans now and we had become quite good at what we did." Urban had developed the reputation among his men that he would never ask them to do anything he wouldn't do. He was not only popular with the men, but respected as well.

Urban's company went next into Sicily. This was their "silent march." The men learned to move quickly and quietly at night, with full camouflage. There wasn't much fighting during this time; Urban and his troops spent most of their time taking ground and avoiding the Germans. Urban developed the nickname *Ghost* because he had learned to rely on deception and avoidance. "Stealth and sweat wins more wars than force and blood ever did," says Urban. "It took us three months moving through sometimes impossible terrain before we finally drove the Germans out of Sicily." Then the men were sent to England to prepare for an even bigger invasion: the full-scale invasion of Western Europe, D-Day.

In England, Urban was promoted to captain. Remembering those days, he says, "We trained hard during our time in England. We all knew we were eventually going to hit the beaches in Europe and we would soon meet the Germans again."

Finally, at D-Day + 4, Urban and his men landed on Utah Beach in Normandy. By the fourth day of the invasion the beach was pretty well cleared out, but there was still enemy shelling going on. Urban's company went inland to reinforce troops who were no more than a mile away. These troops had been stopped cold, with their front line halted along a hedgerow just outside of Renouf, France. It was June 14, 1944.

"When I got there, a bazooka gunner had been shot up pretty

bad and I grabbed his gun," remembers Urban. "The commander was pinned down with the rest of his men." Urban immediately saw how desperate their situation was. This unit was being unmercifully raked with tank and machine-gun fire. Urban called for some men to follow him, and he started to make his way forward into the hedgerows.

Arriving at a position he thought would give him the best chance of seeing the attacking tanks, Urban suddenly stood up, fully exposing himself to the enemy. Taking aim, he fired his bazooka and destroyed the two attacking tanks he could see. "I got them both. Then I was spotted by another Panzer, which started coming at me." Urban tried to leap through a hedgerow just as the Panzer's cannon went off. The blast from the tank's thirty-seven-millimeter gun tore into his leg.

"I refused evacuation and stayed with my men," says Urban. Later that night, Urban's company reached a road junction that was their objective. By now, Urban had to be carried on a litter. The battalion surgeon—a major—came over and started to examine the injured soldier. When he saw how badly injured Urban was, the surgeon said, "Captain, why are you still here? I'm sending you out for immediate evacuation." Urban again refused. But this time the major told him it was an order, and Urban was taken away. He was sent back to a hospital in England.

During the next few weeks while he was recuperating, he could see men from his company coming back wounded. It bothered him that so many were being lost, and he knew that part of the reason was the lack of battle-experienced officers. He had been in the hospital for almost a month, and by now he wanted to get back. But they wouldn't let him go. "I guess I was still having quite a bit of problem walking," admits Urban.

Just outside the hospital, there was a tent city of troops who had left their units and gone AWOL. "These guys were true misfits," remembers Urban. "They would hardly ever say 'sir.' Instead they would address officers saying, 'Yes, boss,' 'No, boss.' They had no discipline." But Urban saw that he might have a use for them.

He went to the colonel in charge and argued that, because of his recreational officer experience, he could work with these men. The colonel was a little surprised that someone would want to do this, but ended up buying the story. He placed Urban in charge of the AWOL soldiers. There were about forty of them.

"First, I just let them go," recalls Urban. "They played dice a lot and they liked to fight each other. Basically, though, they were my prisoners." Over the next two to three weeks, Urban started to introduce some discipline. This wasn't easy since he was the only officer present. It wasn't complete discipline, either; but at least it was something. As Urban tells it, "One time, I even took them to a barber shop and had their hair cut. They sure did a lot of screaming and yelling."

Urban's job, as the Army saw it, was to get these misfits across the English Channel. But really, they were Urban's ticket back to his own men. He remembers, "On our way over the channel to France, some of these guys actually went overboard to escape the fighting! It was incredible."

When Urban finally got most of his changes to the beach at Normandy, he found a lieutenant, returned the officer's salute, and said, "My name is Captain Urban. These men are yours, Lieutenant. Good luck." Before the lieutenant could answer or ask any questions, Urban was gone, headed over a hill as quickly as he could go on his still injured leg. "I didn't want him to figure out what he had while I was still around," says Urban.

Urban quickly found an ambulance that would give him a ride toward Saint-Lô. From there, he found a mail jeep that took him to his unit on the front lines. "I'll never forget the massive numbers of American bombers flying over our heads that day," Urban remembers.

When he finally arrived on the front lines at 1130 hours on July 25, 1944, Operation Cobra had begun just thirty minutes before. There were five divisions spread along a front line that was beginning the Allied attack on Saint-Lô. "I remember coming to a point where some of our tanks were burning on a road and the Germans were raining fire down on exposed Americans. The troops were frozen on their stomachs in fear," Urban recalls. "These guys were actually part of my battalion."

Seeing the dangerous situation, Urban yelled, "Who's in charge here?" No one responded. So, with a self-made crutch waving in one hand and a .45-caliber pistol in the other, Urban screamed out, "You men are dead ducks if you don't move. The Germans are on the ridge, zeroed into this position. Follow me. Let's get out of here." The men scrambled after Matt, repositioning themselves to the right flank, off the road, and out of the line of fire. He now had forty men with him.

Later that day, Urban found his regular company. When he arrived, they were also in a desperate situation, pinned down in a valley with the enemy firing from a ridge overlooking them. Two American support tanks for the company had been destroyed, and another—still intact but without a tank commander or gunner—was stuck in a hedgerow. Matt realized he needed that tank's guns to protect his men's position.

"The tank lieutenant came to me and said he could get the tank moving," Urban recalls. "I said okay and he left, but he was killed as he entered the turret. By now, we were under even heavier fire and I ordered a sergeant to go. He was gunned down, too, just as he reached the tank."

Urban had now seen two of his men die carrying out his orders. He wasn't going to send anyone else to their death, so he decided to go to the tank himself. "I guess my limp leg might have saved me because I crawled like a snake, very slowly, toward that tank and didn't get shot," says Urban. "When I got to the tank, I had to get my head above the turret to man the .50-caliber machine gun. I remember thinking, 'Good-bye, world.' Tears started coming from my eyes like a faucet. 'God help me.' " Then, Urban stood up and started firing the machine gun right into the German positions. "I'm not dead, I'm not dead!'' he kept thinking. Bullets were ricocheting all around him.

A crew now had the tank moving; and with Urban firing the tank's machine gun from the top of the turret, they started moving forward toward an even more exposed position. Inspired by their captain, the men got up and began following behind the tank as it advanced into the enemy. A withering return fire was now being delivered by the Americans, and some of the Germans actually began standing up in disbelief at what they were seeing.

"I guess they couldn't believe I wasn't shot and now this tank was moving against them,'' says Urban. "The Germans went from being the hunters to being the prey, and we just started pulverizing them.'' That day, Urban's company made the farthest advance of the entire Saint-Lô breakthrough. They were finally stopped when over the radio a colonel started yelling, "Hold it, Captain. You're getting too far out front. Consolidate your position.''

A few days later, on August 6, 1944, Matt Urban became the entire 2nd Battalion commander—a job usually given to lieutenant colonels. And he was still only a captain!

Urban's men continued fighting their way across France toward Phillipsville, Belgium, where there was a tributary of the Meuse River. The river here was wide and shallow, and a bridge going over it had been blown up. This was a critical location for the Allied move on to Germany.

Urban's men crossed the river in single file and got into Belgium on the other side. There they set up positions on a slope. Urban had decided they shouldn't move any farther until they could get some heavy-weapons artillery support. "The situation actually became unbelievable,'' remembers Urban. "Here we were in the middle of combat, sitting on a slope in the sunshine, having a picnic.'' Nothing was moving.

The battalion objective was a village about a mile away on a slight rise. Everything stayed quiet and peaceful until a call came over the radio from a colonel who said, "Captain Urban, get going into the village. Get moving." Urban radioed back and said, "Colonel, I can't move until we can get heavy weapons and artillery support."

Just then, Urban saw some Germans approaching in a command car. They were coming across the field in front of Urban's slope, to see where the Americans might be. Urban and his men could see them, but the Germans still hadn't seen the Americans. Urban ordered the men to hold their fire and let the Germans get as close to the river as they wanted. "When they got to us, we gave them a nice welcome," Urban remembers. "They sure were surprised to see us so close."

The Germans stood up in their car when they saw the Americans. Urban's men shouted, "Surrender! Surrender!" The enemy soldiers started to swing their car around to escape, which was a mistake. They were immediately chopped down by American M-1 rifle fire.

One of the men, a Sergeant Evans, brought the command car back to Urban and said, "Cap, we got transportation for you now. You have a car." The guys were proud of what they had done for their captain who was still having trouble walking.

The radio came alive again. This time, the colonel said there was nothing in front of them and they needed to take the village. Again, Matt told the colonel, "I'm not going to turn my men loose on that ridge unless I have artillery support." Matt kept thinking, "Court-martial, court-martial, court-martial." But he had decided this would be better than sending his men to their deaths unnecessarily.

"Since we wouldn't move, the colonel sent a company from another battalion," remembers Urban. "These men passed us marching in columns of two. I remember thinking they must be new because they were in clean uniforms and they didn't look like they knew what they were doing." These troops made it about a half-mile farther toward the village, and then they were annihilated. "It happened so quickly," recalls Urban. "A few of them were able to get back to us, but most of them were wounded or killed. There was nothing we could do to help them."

Later that day, the commanding general called a meeting of battalion commanders. Because of his leg injury, Urban rode to the meeting in the German command car that had been captured earlier in the day. Sergeant Evans insisted on being Urban's driver, even though he had never driven before. "I guess he figured he should drive that car because it was his gift to me," says Urban.

Urban was wearing no insignia when he entered the commander's tent. He was wearing an Air Corps jacket that he had bought earlier by trading a German Luger pistol. "I don't think too many people knew I was just a captain," remembers Urban. "This was a meeting for battalion commanders and up."

The general told the officers that the village of Phillipsville needed to be taken. Then he said, "Colonel Urban." Urban wasn't a colonel, but nevertheless he answered, "Yes, sir." "You have been on the front lines. What would you suggest?" asked the commanding general. Urban told the general that, if he had artillery support, his men could get in there. The general replied, "We'll give you artillery support at 0450, and at 0500 you attack." Phillipsville, Belgium—the gateway to Germany—had just become the captain's responsibility.

"I wanted it. My men wanted it. We wanted that town on the rising slope," remembers Urban. "We had been given the job and we were going to do it. But first I had to get out of there before the general realized he had just given the job to a captain." So, Urban replied, "Yes, sir, General. Thank you, sir." And he turned and left before the general could change his mind.

Sure enough, the officer who had ordered the doomed attack earlier in the day complained to the general, "But, sir, he's only a captain." The general turned toward this colonel, glared, and said, "That's Urban from Africa."

Sergeant Evans and Captain Urban hurried back to their men. All the way, Evans was saying, "Yes, Colonel, sir. No, Colonel, sir." And then when they got back, the rest of the guys started doing the same. They were proud as could be of their "Colonel."

That night, Urban led a scouting patrol into the town. They were not seen, and their only contact was a German sentry who had to be killed with a wire. Urban and his scouts found the town to be well fortified, and the Germans had tanks there. Urban returned to the troops and told them, "We have our work cut out for us, men." The rest of the night was spent putting together the next morning's plan of attack.

At 0450, just before the sun rose, a tremendous ten-minute artillery barrage began. As planned, however, Urban and his men started their way from the Meuse River toward Phillipsville.

"When we hit the town, we got stopped not only by machine gun fire, but also by an antiaircraft gun!" recalls Urban. "I had never seen one used like this before." Moving quickly from his command position to the front of the battalion, Matt Urban could see that this machine gun nest had a full view of the Americans. He quickly reorganized his attacking elements. A sergeant came to him and said, "Captain, let me try to get that gun." Urban replied, "Go."

The sergeant got to within fifty feet of it, but was killed. Urban got up from his position and charged into the enemy gun. "I moved faster than I ever moved before. I threw one grenade and then I threw another one just as I got to where the sergeant had been hit," recalls Urban. The second grenade was a direct hit on the machine gun nest, but it cost him a bullet in the neck. Urban was down.

"I was lying there conscious but bleeding, with a big hole in my neck," remembers Urban. "Another machine gun began firing at me." A private dove down to where his captain was lying and compressed the pulsating neck wound. He wasn't going to let his commander die.

Urban was dragged to a roadside ditch where Major Norman Weinberg, the battalion surgeon, could get to him. A tracheotomy was immediately performed on Urban's neck so he could breathe. Mortar and heavy weapons fire continued to threaten the downed captain. Urban was still conscious when the Catholic chaplain reached him, though. He remembers men crowding around as the chaplain looked over at the doctor and asked, "Any hope?" Everyone turned and looked at the doctor, who shook his head. "Thanks a lot!" Urban thought. "I felt like dying right there."

They draped Urban over the hood of a jeep and started back to the front lines. While his men continued their advance into the village, Urban was headed the other way now, to the field hospital. His part of that battle was over. "My boots had been on for a month," remembers Urban.

Urban's next six weeks were spent in a field hospital tent. And when the doctors saw he wasn't going to die, he was sent to a hospital in England. "Again, I wanted to get back with my men," remembers Urban. "I was recuperating in the hospital, but I couldn't talk. I had absolutely no voice and they wouldn't let me go."

Finally, Urban was able to cajole his doctors into giving him a five-day convalescent pass to Scotland. They figured a few days' rest in the Scottish countryside would do him good. So they gave Urban a pass, and he was instantly gone ... but not to Scotland.

Because of big-band leader Glenn Miller's loss in a plane crash—along with so many GI passengers—no flights over the English Channel were being allowed without orders. "I tried like heck to hitch a ride across that channel," remembers Urban. "I spent two nights sleeping on a bench until I hooked up with some Air Corps guys who were sweethearts." They put the voiceless captain in the middle of six airmen as they made their way to a plane on the flight line. It worked. Urban was able to stow aboard and get to France.

Still unable to talk, Urban made all of his communications by writing notes. He wanted to find his battalion, which was now making its way toward Berlin. Urban hitched rides on trucks, jeeps, and whatever he could find. By the time he got near Amsterdam, he was having a particularly difficult time trying to get a ride to the front. Finally he found a truck driver who read his note, looked up at him, and then said, "You're crazy, man. Hop in." This ride got Matt Urban back with his troops.

"My men were surprised and happy to see me," remembers Urban. "I was happy to see them, too." Urban's men wanted him to stay, and he wanted to stay. But the regimental commander said, "You've had enough." Urban was allowed to stay for five days and then he was sent back. The war was finally over for the captain.

"I'm proud of my service to the country," says Urban. "I always tell young people to 'Walk tall and hold their heads high.' I like to think that's what we did so many years ago."

On July 19, 1980, President Jimmy Carter presented to Matt Urban his country's highest military honor for actions taken during the Allied invasion of Europe. After seven Purple Hearts, two Silver Stars, and three Bronze Stars, Matt Urban finally received the honor he deserved most: the Congressional Medal of Honor.

5.

ROBERT E. SIMANEK

It's Not Blood; It's Bud

Recipients of the Medal of Honor sometimes had no intention of performing a heroic act. They were just doing
their job when presented with special circumstances.
Then and only then—with a job clearly needing to be
done—was an unusual act performed.

Robert Simanek thought he was going on a routine mission when his platoon was attacked. However, a series of
incredible actions on his part, including the near sacrifice
of his life when he intentionally shielded an exploding
grenade, saved the lives of fellow soldiers and placed his
name on the honored list of our nation's greatest heroes.

Robert E. Simanek
Private First Class, U.S. Marine Corps
Korea
17 August 1952

The Korean War had started. Robert Simanek from Detroit, Michigan, knew he was going to be drafted. At first, he thought he would be a National Guardsman, and even signed up. But when he was a little late reporting, they sent the military police after him. He decided these guys weren't for him. So he volunteered for the draft and joined the Marines.

In August 1951, Simanek entered the Marine Corps and was sent to boot camp at Parris Island, South Carolina. "That was the hardest thing I ever did," he remembers. "I was physically in excellent shape. But psychologically, this was tough. In a very short period, I went from a carefree lifestyle to one with total discipline." Simanek stuck with it and came out okay. He learned how to march and he learned how to fight. But most importantly, he learned how to be a Marine.

From boot camp he was sent to Pickle Meadows, California. "This was just west of Reno, in the Sierra Nevada Mountains, and it was cold," remembers Simanek. "This training simulated Korea in midwinter and sometimes it was as cold as thirty-five degrees below zero. Because we couldn't even light fires, this was tough training."

Simanek was finally sent to Korea in April 1952, and assigned to the 2nd Battalion, 5th Regiment, of the famed 1st Marine Division. During his first week in Korea, he had an orientation and was made a Browning Automatic rifleman. He was ready for the war. He saw plenty at his first assignment, Outpost Yoke.

"This was the worst place I had ever been," says Simanek. "I received the Medal of Honor for a particular experience, but my most traumatic experiences were at Outpost Yoke. This assignment took me from being a kid to being a fully mature adult. I guess it was a kind of accelerated maturity."

The outpost was about a mile and a half beyond the main

fighting line, and was indefensible. It was used as an observation point during the day, to grid mortar zones; but each night the American Marines were surrounded by the enemy. "We just wanted to survive until morning," remembers Simanek.

There were twelve men in Simanek's unit. They had a machine gun crew and one radio man. Sometimes they would stay at the outpost overnight, but on other occasions they would stay for several days.

Piper Cub spotter planes would fly over and tell the Marines when large forces of the enemy were coming toward them. When this happened, the Americans would quickly abandon the base until it was safe, and then come back later. The men became experts at searching out booby traps when they returned. "They liked to leave those things for us," remembers Simanek.

Outpost Yoke was set up as a series of two-man bunkers, so the men always shared their foxhole with a buddy. Simanek talks about one time when they came under fire and enemy soldiers started coming up the hill after them. "I was having trouble getting a field of fire through my gun's small aperture, so I left the bunker just as a grenade was thrown inside where I had been. That grenade killed my buddy. When I went back in to check him, another mortar round hit just outside where I had been. I was almost killed again. I started considering life a gift."

Many times, enemy snipers would close in at night, trying to sight an American to kill. The Marines were sometimes reduced to firing back at shadows and sounds. They sprayed back as much as they could, but Simanek's Browning Automatic— although an excellent long-range rifle—was a poor weapon for this type of "close in" combat. A shotgun would have been much better. Simanek did his job the best he could under the circumstances.

While stationed at Yoke, Simanek became friends with another Marine named Donnell Crowder. He was a cook from

Alabama who had volunteered for the front lines. Because
Crowder didn't drink, he would give Simanek his beer ration.
Eventually the two became pretty good friends. "Donnell and
I were selected to complete the base's trenchline perimeter on
its forward exposed ridge," Simanek remembers. "No one had
been able to do this because it was exposed to the enemy. We
tried. We pounded away with our trench tools as quickly as we
could, our rifles always near." While they worked, Crowder
would keep Simanek laughing—to keep both their minds off
the danger. Pretending to hear enemy soldiers coming, Crowder
would start throwing cans (of all things) down the ridge. Eventually, they did indeed get the job done.

"We were proud we completed the ridge perimeter, elimi-
nating a blind approach to the outpost," remembers Simanek.
"No one had been able to do it before. Because we did, our unit
was better able to survive during the coming attacks."

The Outpost Yoke assignment lasted just a few weeks, but
Simanek never forgot the horror of this time in his life. The day
after his unit left the base, their relief troops were overrun. By
the time they could get back to help them, the Chinese had
done their horrible work. Almost half the Marines were dead.
Surprisingly, the wounded were left alone.

"I'll never forget the blood in the trenches when we got
there," Simanek remembers. "There were eight bodies, and I
remember pouring blood over the side from the plastic which
we lined the trenches with. Then we carried the wounded and
dead back to our lines. You never forget this. Those men could
easily have been us."

In this environment of death and sacrifice, Simanek began to
realize the value of life. Every day became an extra for him.
Seeing death so closely made him understand how fragile life
really is. Anyone who knew Outpost Yoke knew combat; Yoke
was Simanek's not-so-gentle easing into war and death.

Simanek started doing patrols—lots of them. Sometimes these
patrols would go as far as three miles behind the enemy lines.

Once, Simanek recalls, a patrol was actually sent out to look for a missing soldier from a previous patrol because the lieutenant forgot to count himself when he did his platoon count.

Later, Simanek's unit was transferred to the Hook Ridge Line. Here the outposts were named after women. Outpost Irene was on the tip of a finger ridge that jutted out from the main ridge line. The Marines called her the "ugly blister." Irene was forward of the main American line; she was used for observing the enemy and plotting out grids for mortar attacks.

Simanek became the platoon's radio man. His job was to stay with the platoon leader and send communications back to the main line. The platoon would go out on patrols in groups of about eighteen men. "We manned these outposts during the day for observation and left them to come back to the main line at night," remembers Simanek. "They would have been too costly to hold at night like we did with Outpost Yoke."

As dangerous as it sounds, this assignment of going to Outpost Irene every morning for a day of observation was comparatively easy. A patrol of men would leave the front-line base camp at first light each morning. Often, Simanek would stick a couple of beers and an old Reader's Digest into his baggy uniform pockets and would head up the ridge to the outpost for a generally pretty boring day of observation. The Chinese usually left the Marines alone on these daily visits.

One day they didn't.

On the morning of August 17, 1952, the Chinese had a well-planned ambush ready for the Marines. What the enemy hadn't planned on was a new sergeant who led the Marine platoon up to Outpost Irene by a way that was different from the usual.

Simanek remembers that morning: "As soon as we could see to walk, we left our main-line base camp. I just got back from an all-night patrol and, because this squad needed a radio man, I had to go. Without any sleep, I really didn't want to. But this was supposed to be an easy run."

The Chinese were waiting for the Americans along their usual route to Outpost Irene. Because the men went a different way this day, though, they walked into the enemy's side, rather than head-on. Luckily, this meant the Marines missed the full effect of the ambush.

"When they opened up, the machine gunner right behind me was instantly killed," Simanek recalls. "Twelve men made a quick dash back down the ridge to the base of the hill. They got away, but six of us dove into a narrow trenchline farther up, for cover." There were enemy soldiers just above and below these Marines' position. An intense firefight began. Several Americans were wounded right away.

Simanek immediately radioed to the main line, reporting they were hit. Because the line of radio contact was not very direct, he had to radio someone at another outpost first, who then repeated the transmission back to the front lines. It took some time to get a response.

The Chinese started throwing grenades. All of a sudden there were a dozen of them in the trenchline. Frantically, the Marines kicked them out. They were nearly successful, except for one that exploded in the trench and tore into Simanek's leg.

"I was firing at the enemy with my .45 pistol," Simanek remembers. "But this wasn't very useful against their automatics. Between the action and the radio relay situation, I was pretty busy."

Even though the Marines had walked more than a mile from the base camp, a portion of the American front line was actually parallel to their trail and close enough for a tank to fire. One was quickly positioned in the rough terrain as close as it could get to the trapped Marines. Simanek started to direct the tanker's fire. He remembers, "The tank was firing shells as fast as it could. Finally, we got a hit on the bunker below us. Now we could get back to our main line."

Then two more grenades flew into the trenchline. Simanek was able to throw one away, but he saw he couldn't get rid of the other grenade in time. Realizing the danger to the other Marines, he fell sideways on the grenade and jammed it into the dirt with his thigh. It went off.

"The blast penetrated my leg from the right hip to the knee," Simanek remembers. "I began losing a lot of blood, but my wounds seemed *especially* wet. Then they started to smell like beer. Soon I realized the can of beer in my pocket had been blown apart, along with my *Reader's Digest* and the rest of my leg. During all this, I actually remember feeling angry about losing that beer! I guess you could say, 'It wasn't blood; it was Bud...'"

Simanek was down. His legs were useless now. He started wrapping bandages around his wounds as best he could while continuing to give artillery reports to the tank. The tank kept up its artillery barrage under Simanek's direction. A Marine P-51 flashed overhead and started dropping napalm on the hill. A rescue team was trying to reach the trapped Marines, but it had to withdraw because of intense enemy fire coming from the higher bunker.

Simanek stayed on his radio, giving artillery instructions to the tank. The American fire was getting more accurate. Finally, the rescue team returned and started carrying wounded men down the hill. Simanek was being helped by two men just as a tank shell from the American tank hit them. "One of the guys carrying me had his shoulder shot off," Simanek recalls. "I could see bone. The other guy was hit in the hip. I was hit in the face. The situation was crazy."

Simanek yelled, "Leave me. Get back as far as you can!" The wounded rescuers left as the shelling slowed. Simanek started crawling down the hill behind everyone else. He could hear instructions come over his radio, ordering him to keep his head down. "Just stay there and keep down. We're going to kill everything on the hill behind you." Simanek believed them. It seemed like everything on the hill was under fire.

Simanek remembers, "I saw a machine gunner ahead, who I thought was covering me. I crawled to him and told him to stay down. Then I realized he wasn't talking back to me. He was dead."

By now, Simanek was exhausted. He had lost a lot of blood

and was barely awake. He remembers his helicopter ride out of there, but little else.

Robert Simanek spent the next six months in a hospital, learning how to walk again. He suffered from palsy of the peroneal nerve. Even after he was able to walk again, he could only shuffle. But he knew he was lucky to be alive.

Looking back at this time, Simanek says, "I really can't say I was afraid on that ridge. At least it wasn't uncontrollable or destructive fear. Part of this may have been from incredible fatigue, but part of it was my awareness about how a Marine is supposed to act. I think I started fulfilling some of those expectations that day."

Many other people thought so, too. On October 23, 1953, President Dwight D. Eisenhower presented to Robert Simanek the Congressional Medal of Honor, this country's highest award.

6.

FRED WILLIAM ZABITOSKY

Against the Odds

Medal of Honor recipients will often describe their Medal action by saying, "I was just doing my job." If so, it would be reasonable to say that the recipients were very good at their jobs—whether flying planes, running riverboats, or conducting long-range "recon" patrols.

One of the best at his job was "Green Beret" Fred Zabitosky. He served four Southeast Asia tours in the Army Special Forces; and by the time he was done, few people knew how to operate long-range patrols better than he did. Not only were Fred Zabitosky's experience and ability producing mission successes, they also were saving lives. Zabitosky's job well done caused this Green Beret to receive a Medal of Honor.

Fred William Zabitosky
Staff Sergeant, U.S. Army
Laos
19 February 1968

Born October 27, 1942, Fred Zabitosky grew up with little discipline. Vandalism and petty theft had made him experienced with the juvenile home in Trenton, New Jersey, while an unhappy home life had him running away frequently. Trouble was something he was quite familiar with.

When Zab's six-year-old brother died of lockjaw in the early 1950s, his dad started to drink heavily. This drinking led to the loss of a business and any financial security the family might have had. Zab remembers asking his dad for a new coat one winter, and being told no. "Just wear two shirts," his dad said.

Zab envied kids with bicycles. He didn't have one, and his family couldn't afford to buy him one. He couldn't even join the Boy Scouts: the uniforms cost too much. Things weren't going well for the Zabitosky family.

In high school, other kids laughed at Zab because he couldn't read or spell. He had never learned how to, in grade school. As one of the only white kids in an all-black school, he had never learned another thing: prejudice. His first girlfriend was black. People have always just been people to Zab; growing up, he didn't recognize the difference between blacks and whites.

Because he wasn't good at school, he got from the streets whatever sense of self-worth he had. But one of his friends went to the electric chair. A number of them ended up in prison. Zab was headed there, too.

Things got worse. When Zab was only fifteen, his father left home. Zab was forced to become the man of the family. His mother had no money to raise Zab's younger brothers and sisters. Already used to having very little—growing up in a poor Polish community—they now had even less. Zab was forced to take on responsibilities for the first time in his life.

He did.

Initially, he took jobs after school as well as helping take care of the younger children in the family. "It kind of bothered me that we didn't have more than we did," recalls Zab. "My major goal in life had been to get away from the arguments. But after my father deserted us in 1957, it became the survival of my mother, little brother, and sisters."

Eventually, Zab was forced to quit school to support the family. He took on odd jobs, including two paper routes and a stint unloading the fishing ships in the harbor. Zab worked hard and took on more and more responsibility.

Even though his family was surviving, Zab realized he wasn't getting anywhere in his own life. His responsibilities taught him to start looking at the future, and he didn't like what he saw.

"I always had respect for military people," Zab recalls. "I saw them in parades and I thought they looked good in uniform. I decided the military might be a good chance for me to complete high school and then establish goals for myself. It might even become a career." Besides, Zab figured, he had always been a leader of the delinquents!

Seventeen years old when he joined the Army in 1959, Zab immediately found the home he never had before. "I loved the discipline and I loved the pride," remembers Zab. "This was the first time I ever experienced either."

Zab trained in Fort Benning, Georgia. Basic training was the first time he had ever been out of the New Jersey area. After basic, he was sent to Europe. He took a lot of pride in his assignments. When he was a kid, everything had been divided into black and white, good and bad, Protestant and Catholic, rich and poor. In the Army, these easy divisions weren't always as clear as they seemed when Zab was growing up.

While in the military, Zab continued his support for his mother, brother, and two sisters. Forty of his sixty-eight dollars of pay were sent to them each month. In fact, throughout his career, he always sent his mother at least half of what he made.

Zab's family life had been very hard. So it was not much of

a shock to him when he realized Army life was a no-nonsense life, too. "We worked no less than six and a half days per week," Zab recalls. "There were no passes. We got up at 0500 each morning, did physical training, and then ate breakfast. After this, we had a personal and barracks inspection. If you had a deficiency, you were in trouble. After work, we would scrub the barracks down and go to bed. The next day was the same."

There was no recreation. In fact, Zab only had a single three-day pass during his entire two and a half years in Germany—and that was for being named Outstanding Soldier of the Month! During his entire time there, he went downtown only three times. But he didn't mind the discipline, and he didn't mind the work. The Army took the Soviet threat seriously, and Zab took the Army seriously.

During his three years in the Army, Zab advanced from E-1 to E-4 and graduated from high school. When his tour ended, he received a good conduct medal with letters of commendation. And the Army wanted him to stay on. They even offered him an E-5 promotion to reenlist.

Zab missed his family and wanted to see what the world outside the Army was like. So when his time was up, Zab went back to New Jersey and took construction jobs. He continued supporting his family, though he wasn't even earning enough money to buy a used car. He asked his boss if he could start working on Saturdays and Sundays too. The boss looked at him suspiciously and said okay.

It was on one of those Sundays, when Zab had been out of the Army for three months, that he started thinking. "Here you are back as a laborer. While you were in the military, you were a leader. You were paid monthly and you stood a chance of advancing higher in your career." Zab wanted his self-respect back. He realized he had found a home with the older non-commissioned officers who were his substitute fathers. He decided the best thing to do was to go back into the military and make it a career. In January 1963, he did just that. He made the right decision.

Zab decided he wasn't going to be a regular soldier. He wanted to go into the Airborne because he had always looked with respect on the parachute-qualified troops in the 24th Division. He wanted to be like them. They were professional, sharp, and—at least the ones he had seen—cared about their jobs. He still didn't know what the Special Forces were, but he was about to learn.

Zab went to airborne and jump school in Fort Benning, Georgia. At the end of the program, Special Forces recruiters arrived on the scene, asking if anyone wanted to be tested. Zab wanted to be included, and so his testing began. Only about 5 percent of the men who met the selection criteria actually made it into Green Beret training, and only half of these made it into the Green Berets.

Zab made it. Then he started advanced training in field survival courses, ambush techniques, small unit tactics, airborne operations, the setting up of landing zones, sea operations, and unconventional warfare. This training taught Zab how to give military instruction—a Special Forces team's main program and mission. In addition, Zab learned how to infiltrate behind enemy lines to supply and equip guerillas.

Green Beret training lasted seven months. During this time, Zab also went to communications school. He was becoming something very special for the first time in his life.

"I was as proud to be Special Forces qualified and wear that Green Beret as I am to wear the Medal of Honor now," says Zab. "This was a very elite corps; only a small number of men can actually wear the Green Beret." In 1963, Zab completed Special Forces training at Fort Bragg, North Carolina. He was assigned to Special Forces A-Team.

A-Team was an operational detachment consisting of ten enlisted men and two officers. Zab was the youngest man on the team. The men stayed together all the time, whether they were in a jungle battle or a Carolina bar. These men's lives depended on each other, and they loved each other like brothers.

Zab's first mission sent him to Alaska, where the team lived with the Eskimos. "We stayed up there with Eskimo National Guard Scouts for four months," says Zab. "We lived with them and trained with them in intelligence and infiltration methods."

After Alaska, Zab and his unit came back to the States and trained as a counterinsurgency team. During this time—in 1964—Zab was married. But by September, the unit was ready for Vietnam. They were sent on a six-month training mission with the 5th Special Forces Group. When they got there, however, the unit's plan changed from a six-month to a one-year tour. Zab's only problem was how he was going to tell his new wife.

"I wasn't scared in Vietnam, because I was confident," Zab recalls. "This is what I had been trained for in Special Forces. It was simply a continuation of my training and it was my job."

The Green Berets' mission was to organize the Montagnard mountain tribesmen. Special Forces accomplished this mission by treating the Montagnards with respect. The Green Berets lived like the Montagnards and helped them medically and educationally. They gave them clothes and weapons. The Montagnards and the Green Berets developed a special relationship, which created a buffer zone that hindered the North Vietnamese from infiltrating into South Vietnam.

In February 1965, Zab went out on a security patrol with two Montagnard companies. They saw smoke rising from the jungle in the Mang-Yang Pass. Zab asked one of his Montagnard guides what the smoke was, and was told it was the Vietminh. Zab informed Sergeant First Class Billy Carrow, his American partner on the mission, that he would take a company out to check the smoke.

When the company approached the smoke, they walked right into an ambush. Zab was the only American; this was the first time he had ever been under enemy fire.

The Montagnards were frightened, and some started to retreat. Zab returned fire, trying to break contact with the enemy. Montagnards were being shot, but most held their ground. Zab radioed back to Billy for mortar support. The shells started falling. One of the Montagnard guides ran to Zab and showed him a Chinese weapon that had just been taken off a dead enemy soldier—a soldier wearing the green uniform of the North Vietnamese Army.

Zab pulled the men back, and a Green Beret relief force was called in. During the debriefing that followed this action, the North Vietnamese contact was reported. This was the war's first NVA confirmation. Even General William Westmoreland came for the debriefing, taking the captured Chinese weapon back with him as proof of the North Vietnamese involvement.

The war was cranking up. The enemy began attacking towns and camps, trying to induce the Army of the Republic of Vietnam (ARVN) 23rd Division down through the Mang-Yang Pass where it could be ambushed. The enemy hit the towns pretty hard, and the Special Forces camps throughout the area became pretty busy.

Zab's camp supported five Montagnard battalions consisting of sixteen hundred tribesmen. Their job became the increasingly difficult one of securing the road across Mang-Yang Pass. Once, while the men were on a patrol mission, the NVA hit their base outpost and killed fifty Montagnards. "We lost twenty-six of our trucks, and people were captured," remembers Zab.

During this time, the Americans started flying the first bombing missions of the war. This period was the beginning of the first large-scale battle American troops fought against the North Vietnamese. By February 1965, Zab was smack in the middle of a war. His experience as a combat soldier had begun.

When it was time for Zab to rotate back to the United States in September, he was ready. He hadn't seen his wife in a year, and he now had a baby boy. He was proud of that year in Vietnam. He had led many combat operations, and his confidence as a Green Beret had matured. The team of twelve men went back to Fort Bragg where their training continued. But the paperwork they had to complete—a record of their year in the field—was just beginning. A whole year's worth of "after-action reports" was enough to make any combat soldier want to go back. Zab did, seven months later, in April 1966.

He volunteered to go to Vietnam with the 5th Special Forces Group on a "special project." All the volunteers were senior NCOs with combat experience. These were handpicked Green Berets. As for Zab's wife, she accepted this as part of his job; she knew he had chosen Special Forces, even before they were married.

Zab was assigned to MAC-V SOG (military studies and observation group—Vietnam), which operated intelligence-gathering missions in three areas: North Vietnam, Laos, and Cambodia. These missions had been secretly run since 1961.

The group fell under the direct command of General Westmoreland, the chairman of the Joint Chiefs of Staff, and the Commander in Chief of Pacific Operations (CINC-PAC). Zab's project—called Operation 34—was designed to train South Vietnamese agents and infiltrate them into the North. His job was to teach these agents advanced parachute operations, demolitions, and communications. The infiltrators received up to one and a half years of training. Then they were sent to North Vietnam to set up and send out information on the enemy.

When these agents were inserted into North Vietnam, they were given sophisticated radio communications equipment and the training necessary to create misinformation. Unfortunately, many times when these people hit the ground, they would turn on the Americans. The "agents" for this project either came from North Vietnam or else were South Vietnamese with criminal records—those facing long jail terms or death sentences. Often their incentive for cooperating was that family members would be well taken care of during their "duty."

Zab stayed in Vietnam for a year, conducting these operations. He was stationed outside Saigon, where military formalities didn't exist. His special group never wore uniforms; and because they were all basically the same rank, divisions of responsibility were pretty equal between the members. The training groups consisted of Air Commandos, SEALs, and Green Berets.

One time, a South Vietnamese prisoner who had been released and sent through the training program was under the control of a CIA case officer. The agent was nearly ready for insertion. Because such agents utilized top secret monitoring devices, the Special Forces instructors hated to see them go bad after they were inserted. The week before this particular agent was due to infiltrate, he went AWOL for a short time. Zab found him and told his CIA case officer that the man was a poor risk and shouldn't be sent. The case officer didn't appreciate Zab's comments, but he had to respond to them. Zab was called before the U.S. ambassador, Ellsworth Bunker, to explain himself. Zab gave Ambassador Bunker his reasons for wanting the agent removed from the program, but he was overruled.

The Vietnamese agent was deployed on Christmas Eve, during a Christmas cease-fire. Zab remembers that Christmas morning: "We all woke up with radio reports blaring, 'Breach of the cease fire. An agent was infiltrated on Christmas morning.' The man turned himself over to the enemy as soon as he landed."

In April 1967, Zab was back at Fort Bragg. Again, though, a life of raking leaves, cleaning the base, and filling out reports was not the kind of duty he wanted: eventually the appeal of returning to Vietnam became more than he could resist. "I decided to volunteer for a third tour in Vietnam," Zab recalls. "Again, I was assigned to special projects."

It was September 1967. Zab was back with MAC-V SOG—this time assigned to Op Project 35, also known as "Shining Brass." The project went by the code name *Prairie Fire* when referring to its secret operations into Laos. These operations had been going on for two years. Zab's mission was to infiltrate across the Laotian and Cambodian borders and monitor the Ho Chi Minh Trail.

Some of these missions required him to set up wiretaps in which NVA telephone lines would be found and monitored.

Other times, Zab would go on mining missions, or on "enemy snatches" to interrogate NVA soldiers. Sometimes he and other members of the team would go into Laos to direct air strikes against enemy troop concentrations and supply depots along the Ho Chi Minh Trail. Other missions had them salting enemy ammunition with booby traps. "We put explosives in their mortar rounds to give them something to think about when they started shooting at Americans," says Zab. "Maybe their next round would blow up. We got pretty good at setting booby traps."

MAC-V SOGs had Green Beret "spike" and "recon" teams. Zab was made the leader of a spike team that consisted of three Americans and nine indigenous troops—usually mercenary Chinese Nungs. The Americans consisted of the team leader, one assistant team leader, and a radio operator; the Nungs were ethnic Chinese who had migrated to Vietnam after World War II. They were pretty good soldiers.

Because the teams were in an unconventional warfare mode, the men wore no uniforms. In fact, they either wore North Vietnamese clothes or generic military fatigues without name tags or any other identification. Their weapons were not American. The rifles were either Soviet AK-47s or Swedish K-submachine guns. The men carried North Vietnamese combat gear and only ate Vietnamese food. Before a mission, they didn't wash for several days, because they didn't want to smell like Americans.

Zab's unit was stationed in Vietnam even though his missions were in Laos. This project was completely controlled by Americans. The White House, the CINC-PAC, and the American Embassy in Laos had to preapprove all missions: the Vietnamese command wasn't involved in the process at all.

Sometimes during missions, whole Special Forces teams would disappear. The enemy never kept prisoners. The men knew this was dangerous work: if they got "policed up" or captured by the enemy, they were lost. There was nothing anybody could do for them. There would be no artillery support and no reinforcements. Because the missions were classified as top secret, the Green Berets knew they were alone. Like everyone else, Zab knew that if he was caught he wouldn't come back. He also knew his family wouldn't be told any of the circumstances of his death, and they probably would never get his body back.

"Every one of this tour's missions were striking, and we saw combat on every one of them," Zab recalls. "Overall on this tour, I had fifteen border-crossing patrols—and you were only supposed to do six. I was getting pretty good at this."

It was during this tour that Zab met Staff Sergeant Doug Glover. "Glover was a very likable guy, but he had never been in combat," remembers Zab. "He arrived in Vietnam and was assigned to my spike team 'Maine.' We were stationed in Kontum at Forward Operational Base #2."

Glover went on his first mission the day after he arrived in country. He was shown where he was going to sleep, and then immediately briefed. The next day the team loaded onto two helicopters. There were three Americans and nine indigenous Nungs. The mission was a recon of an NVA regimental command post.

The UH-1H Huey helicopters crossed the border into Laos. They flew twenty-five miles in, with a forward air controller (FAC) aircraft and two A-1E Skyraider prop fighter escorts. Zab remembers, "We started into the landing zone. When the first chopper—with Glover, me, and half the team—landed, there were four NVA machine guns waiting for us. Glover and both pilots were immediately hit. In fact, the helicopter had over one hundred hits in just seconds."

The A-1E gunships—seeing the trouble—started down to help. It was chaos. The hit helicopter smoked back up and headed out. "The first Skyraider blew in and was hit as it was diving," Zab recalls. "It smashed into the landing zone and blew up with a full load of ordnance." The other Skyraider followed and got hit too, but was able to fly back and crash-land at a Special Forces camp. Zab and Glover's smoking helicopter just barely got back.

This was a typical Green Beret SOG mission. But it was Glover's first combat. Even though he had only been in country for one day, he was already wounded and out of the picture for a while.

Zab continued on missions while Glover was recovering. By the time Glover was ready for his second mission, Zab was still team leader of spike team Maine.

At the battle of Dak To in November 1967, the NVA were using elephants on Hill 875 to carry their supplies. Zab's team, with Glover as assistant team leader, had been on a five-day recon inside Laos. Walking down a trail, they saw a wild elephant ahead of them. The elephant saw them too, and started charging. "The elephant knocked me down and kept chasing the rest of the team," Zab recalls. "The team scattered while this rogue elephant started tromping us. The elephant was out to kill us—and Glover got it again." This time the elephant stomped on Glover's foot, leaving him lying on the ground screaming with pain from his second injury in two missions.

The rest of the team was still running through the bushes, but they eventually regrouped. Doug Glover had to be evacuated. "That night I tied myself in a tree to sleep because I was more worried about elephants than Vietnamese," Zab remembers.

When the team finally got back to base, they checked in on Glover, who was recovering nicely. Zab got "black water fever" on this mission, and he needed some rest, too. During this time, he and the rest of the team really started to develop an affection for Doug Glover. "He hadn't really been with us very long, but we really started getting close to him. He was a hell of a nice guy," recalls Zab.

By now, Zab had run twelve missions into Laos. The Special Forces base commander felt Zab had done enough. The commander decided the team should be turned over to Doug Glover, who was now recovered from his elephant injuries. But because Glover had only been on two missions and had been injured on both of them, Zab was concerned for his friend. Glover didn't yet have the confidence needed to take over. And besides, the team's radio man was also going to be a brand new man. This wasn't a good situation, and both Glover and Zab knew it.

It was February 18, 1968. The Tet Offensive had begun almost three weeks before. The NVA were attacking the major cities of South Vietnam, and they were using Laos and Cambodia as their staging areas. Because the rules of engagement signed at Geneva restricted American troops from going after the enemy over the borders, only the MAC-V SOG Green Berets could go after them. The big question that needed to be answered by reconnaissance was whether there was going to be a second enemy offensive.

A decision was made to infiltrate five MAC-V SOG teams into Cambodia and Laos to determine the enemy's troop concentrations. But because the helicopters were busy with the Tet Offensive, few were available for the Green Beret insertions. The teams had to move across the border one at a time.

Talking the night before the mission, Glover told Zab, "I'm going to get killed. I had a dream. I know I'm going to die tomorrow." Zab responded, "Doug, I'll go in with you." Zab went to the commander and requested permission to be Glover's assistant team leader on the next day's mission. The commander said okay.

The next day, two helicopters carrying the team landed east of Attopeu, Laos. Moving through ten-foot-tall elephant grass and bamboo thickets, Zab could see Glover wasn't very comfortable and—with only two previous missions' experience—wasn't very confident, either. The radio operator, for his part, had never called an air strike.

The men started into the jungle and suddenly realized they were in the middle of an NVA complex. K-wire and bunkers were everywhere. But the real hint was the sight of all those enemy soldiers sitting at their campsites, eating. Just as the team members realized where they were, the NVA realized it too. All of a sudden, guns were firing from both sides. The team started dropping back.

Zab asked Glover what he wanted to do. Glover responded, "You take over the team. You got to take over the team." Zab responded, "All right, move the men back to the landing zone and I'll stay here and cover." The team withdrew. "I wanted them out of there. I had my hands full and I work better alone," remembers Zab. "The team had a better chance to survive at the landing zone."

Zab only had a hand radio in his pocket, and the NVA were coming forward. He was shooting his CAR 15-mini M-16 with its foldable stock. He started setting claymore mines connected to white phosphorus willy-peter grenades as he withdrew. He radioed Doug Glover to call in air strikes on the white smoke as soon as they started going off. Zab knew that an A-1E strike force was on the way.

When Glover saw the smoke from the phosphorous grenades start to blow, he called the bombers in. Zab had no way to communicate directly with the aircraft himself, and now 750-pound bombs and napalm were dropping all around him. Dozens of NVA were fighting toward him.

"I made it back to the landing zone with the rest of the squad, but there were no helicopters yet," Zab recalls. It turned out that all four inserted special-operations teams were in trouble that day, and no helicopters were available to get Zab's team out. Realizing they would have to buy time, Zab positioned each man around a tight perimeter defense just outside the landing zone. Using air support along with an intense machine gun and grenade defense, the Green Berets were able to hold their position. "We were told on the radio to fight until helicopters could get there to pull us out," Zab remembers. "They didn't need to tell us that."

Glover was the radio man now and he worked the air with the A-1Es and their bombs. The forward air controller airplane, flying above the surrounded troops, asked if there were any more Americans outside the defended area. When he was told no, he called the A-1Es even closer, creating a scorching ring of fire. Napalm, 750-pound bombs, and cluster-bomb sets were dropped on the surrounded Green Beret's perimeter.

The Green Berets were experiencing a full frontal assault by three NVA companies, and a fourth company was coming down the hills toward them. Every man was throwing hand grenades, and automatic weapons were firing from everywhere. The claymore mines that Zab had set during his withdrawal were finding targets, but still there were no rescue helicopters.

"This was where we would make our stand," Zab remembers. "There was nowhere else to go." The NVA kept attacking with wave after wave of frontal assaults. Over the next one and a half hours, the overhead FAC aircraft counted twenty-two separate attacks made by the enemy. Zab's team was running out of ammo. The forty-five magazines of bullets each soldier had carried were nearly used up, and the ten hand grenades each man carried were almost gone. The gunships kept ringing the area.

Finally, some "slicks" (stripped-bare helicopters) became available. These were unarmed utility helicopters designed to carry as many troops as possible. Two came over the team, with a third circling above. Medic Luke Nance was in the third helicopter.

The slicks informed the team they couldn't bring the ships down on their landing zone: it was too hot. The team was ordered to a new LZ about five hundred meters away. Zab recalls, "The air strikes were increased to blow a hole for us to get through to the new area."

The NVA continued attacking. "We had been in battles this intense before, but none so prolonged," recalls Zab. "I was still in charge, and I was standing and trying to direct our fire and movement to the new LZ. When you are in charge, your men look to you for guidance and you don't want them to know you are as scared as they are." Zab knew his time was running out along with their ammunition and luck.

The team kept moving toward the second landing zone. The American air attackers increased their barrage on the surrounding enemy, allowing Zab and his men to reach the clearing just as the first slick landed. Zab ordered two Nungs and one American onto the helicopter.

The NVA were figuring out the plan when the first helicopter took off just as the second landed. The enemy regouped and started moving toward the new position. Zab's team kept firing. It looked like they were going to make it out, even though it would be close. Glover looked at Zab, smiled through his dirty face and said, "You brought us through again, Zab." Zab replied, "You see, you had nothing to worry about with that dream. I dreamed I was going to be wounded, and that didn't happen either."

The six remaining team members ran to the open door of the second helicopter. Zab ran to the left side, firing his gun, while the other men got in on the right. The NVA were getting closer, and Zab hung out the door, still firing his gun as the helicopter took off. The helicopter's machine gunners were firing too. But all of a sudden, the ship exploded when a rocket-propelled grenade hit it in the tail. "There was a violent jolt followed by screaming," Zab remembers. "I saw the tail boom come around and I heard an explosion. Then I remember falling. It was like a dream." The helicopter crashed.

Zab landed about twenty feet from the burning wreckage. He was on fire and, in his dream, he remembers thinking that he was near a very hot sun. When he started coming to, he realized that the "hot sun" was the melting helicopter and that he was in the fight of his life. His clothes were on fire and he could hear screams coming from the downed chopper. Zab knew he was hurt. His first thought was, "Don't let them catch you or they'll kill you." He wanted to crawl into the bush and maybe be rescued. But he heard the screams from the chopper again.

The ship's fuel cells and ordnance were going off. Zab knew five of his team were still in that bird, along with two pilots and two machine gunners. He was the only one thrown from the helicopter, which had broken at midsection and twisted on its right side. "I was out of ammunition, and the gun barrel of my rifle was bent from the fall," Zab remembers. "Now, all of a sudden, I'm faced with the reality of losing my whole team. I was hurting bad."

The MAC-V SOG rules said that aircrew needed to be taken care of before Special Forces team members—in all situations. The aircrew had priority, so Zab fought his way into the cockpit and started dragging the dazed pilot out first. The ship was melting, and Zab had broken his back and several ribs. He remembers, "I dragged the pilot out and saw he was awake. The helicopter was exploding. I asked him to help me get the copilot, who was still screaming. The pilot refused, saying it was too late and there was no chance the copilot could live. He left me, dragging my bent gun with him."

Above the crash site was Green Beret medic Luke Nance in one of the rescue helicopters. "We were receiving fire and I saw Zab's helicopter go down. It was exploding, but I thought I saw something move just outside." The pilots were convinced nothing survived the crash, and they were ready to get out of there. But Nance went to the cockpit and demanded, "No, we're not leaving. We're going down there to see if we can find anyone alive." Nance had his armaments on. The pilots realized this Green Beret meant what he said. There was still the possibility that men were alive, and they were going down to see.

Nance's helicopter came down about sixty meters away from the crash site, and the injured pilot started crawling toward them. "We went down but didn't land," Nance remembers. "I jumped out of the chopper and shot an NVA point blank out of a tree. There was a lot of fire and there were NVA troops coming at us. I could see our men still alive, and I wanted to get to them."

Zabitosky started into the burning helicopter again. The NVA continued their attack, while the copilot kept yelling, "Help me! Please, help me!"

"I made my way inside the cockpit and was able to get to his side," Zab remembers. "I felt my face and shirt burning." The last fuel cell blew as Zab started dragging the copilot out. "We were thrown clear. Landing, we were both on fire. I started dragging him toward the chase copter. He only had a leather pistol belt left on. Everything else was burned off. This guy had melted." Zab remembers the copilot saying to him, "Thanks for not leaving me. Are we going to make it?" Zabitosky replied, "I really don't think so, but we'll try."

The only weapons Zab had left were a pistol and one hand grenade. The NVA had been held outside the LZ perimeter by the intense air support. But now some NVA were starting to get through. Zab remembers, "I pulled the pin on my hand grenade and was ready to just let it blow. But at the last second, I threw it toward some attacking soldiers."

Zabitosky put the copilot on his shoulder. With crushed ribs and a broken back, he made his way toward the chase helicopter. On the way he saw the pilot, who was still on his hands and knees. "I considered leaving him, but I didn't. I started dragging him too," Zab recalls. "We got within ten feet of the rescue ship and I remember Luke Nance's skinny little hands coming to my rescue, grabbing these men and then me. He saved my life." By this time, Zabitosky was tightening up. His injuries were starting to slow him down.

Nance remembers, "I was so happy Zab was alive. I did the best I could under tough circumstances, and that means more than anything."

After Nance grabbed Zab and pulled him into the chopper, Zab passed out and was evacuated to Pleiku, South Vietnam, where he stayed in the hospital for six weeks. Several hundred enemy soldiers were killed that day, including 109 later counted at the first landing zone. The crashed helicopter's two machine gunners—SP-4 Melvin C. Dye and SP-4 Robert S. Griffith—and three indigenous Nungs died in the crash. The copilot died two days later in a hospital major-burn unit. Glover also died in the crash: his dream came true. None of these men were ever recovered from Laos.

This Medal of Honor mission occurred on Zab's third tour. He did return home afterward. It wasn't long though, before he was back in Southeast Asia for his fourth tour—this time with the Rangers assigned to the 101st Airborne Division.

But for one of the most amazing warriors of the Vietnam War, even this wasn't enough. "From 1981 to 1982, I went back into Laos to investigate the possible existence of POW–MIAs for a private organization," says Zabitosky. "I know there were still living POWs in Laos, but I couldn't say whether there are any alive now. There was only one POW who was ever returned from Laos, but there were 668 missing by the end of the war.

"There is no such thing as patriotism in a combat situation. You don't think about medals, promotions, or even the flag. You don't think about why you are there or even your family. You think strictly about the people you are with, and what you can do for each other. You'd be willing to give your life for your fellow soldier—because of your love for him, but also because of your own self-respect.

"I've thought about what would have happened if I didn't go back into that burning helicopter. I still had something left in me, and I wasn't dead yet. Someday I would have had to face the question of whether I did everything I could. Now I can say I did, and that feels pretty good.

"I was presented and I wear the Medal, but it was earned by Doug Glover, my indigenous team members, and all the Special Forces enlisted men who served on special projects. All the guys who wore that Beret in combat have done just as much as I have, even though they haven't received the Medal of Honor."

Zabitosky was notified of his selection for the Congressional Medal of Honor in January 1969. Two months later, President Richard Nixon presented the medal for this classified mission even though the details of the mission could not then be discussed. The Green Berets had received their Medal of Honor.

7.

REGINALD R. MYERS

The Marine

When a man is being shot at thousands of miles from his home—with no thanks and little recognition—his pride and the group's tradition become important. History has recognized the U.S. Marine Corps as a very select military outfit and one of the most effective fighting organizations ever. To become a Marine, one must have a clear understanding of the history and traditions of the corps—an understanding that builds pride, respect, and a sense of honor. When needed, these characteristics can serve a man well. Reg Myers was a Marine who understood the traditions of the corps, and lived them—through his Medal of Honor action and later on, throughout his career.

Reginald R. Myers
Major, U.S. Marine Corps
Near Hagaru-ri, Korea
26–29 November 1950

All Reg Myers and his brother ever wanted to do was to be in the military.

Though he was born in Boise, Idaho, his family moved to Salt Lake City in 1931 when Reg was twelve years old. Reg's older brother was the kind of student who stood out from the rest. He became the ROTC cadet colonel at East High School; and when he graduated, Idaho Senator William E. Borah appointed him to attend West Point. The family couldn't have been more proud of this son, but Reg may have been the proudest of them all.

During his preadmission physical exam, it was discovered that Reg's brother had a wisdom tooth that needed to be removed. He was sent to a dentist, who did the extraction. An infection developed, however, and bacteria spread into his blood. A fever started. And because there weren't very many antibiotics back then, Reg's brother continued to get worse. Four days later he died. It was 1932, and Reg's brother had been only seventeen years old.

"I had a deep affection for my brother," says Reg. "His death was a crushing thing to me. I became dedicated because of my brother's death. I wanted to fulfill his objective."

Reg decided to follow in his brother's footsteps. When it was time for him to go to college, he went to the University of Idaho and joined the ROTC. By the time Reg Myers was a junior, he became cadet colonel just like his brother had, in high school. When he graduated in 1941, he was given an appointment in the Army Air Corps. His first assignment was to the administrative side of a warehouse in Sacramento.

Myers remembers, "While there, I had a master sergeant who was always drunk. Because of his drunkenness, I blistered his tail end." What Myers wasn't expecting was the Army's unusual situation in which active-duty ranks for soldiers can be different from their reserve ranks. Well—as luck would have it—since the war was gearing up, this same master sergeant's unit was called up and he became a reserve major assigned to the warehouse. "This guy went from being my subordinate to being my commander," says Myers. "It soon became clear to me that a change would be desirable; and when a Marine commission became available, I took it." It was August 1941.

In September, he went back to basic officer training, this time in the Marines. By June 1942, Myers was ready for combat duty, and he was assigned to the Marine detail on the USS *New Orleans*. He saw his first action a few months later in the battle of Tasafarongo. "This was one of the first naval actions of the war in this area of the world," recalls Myers. "We were in the New Hebrides, just north of Australia, with five Cruisers following each other. At 11 p.m., the Japanese had their destroyers lay down a pattern of torpedoes." One of these torpedoes hit the *New Orleans*, and 150 feet of her bow was blown off. Out of a crew of 800 men, 205 of Myers's shipmates died.

"I remember being in shock," says Myers. "My ship was sinking and the captain was yelling, 'Abandon ship! Abandon ship!' The second in charge, Commander Riggs, while running to the aft control, saw the ship could be saved and countermanded the captain's order. We were eventually able to secure the ship by going backwards, rather than going forward into the gaping hole."

The ship was grounded at a beach in Tulagi, and repairs were started.

"There, the captain and the commander got into a pretty big fight," remembers Myers. "The captain, even though he had been wrong, had the commander reassigned to a freighter. His career in the Navy was destroyed." When the commander left the ship, the crew respectfully lined up on the deck and saluted him as he walked off. As many as could do so also shook his hand. None of the crew were thinking good thoughts about the captain that day.

To save the ship and get it to a port where it could be properly repaired, the men put palm logs on the bow and closed the hole as much as they could. Then the ship was pulled off the beach and started heading backward toward Sydney, Australia, with a destroyer escort.

When the ship arrived in Sydney, women lined up on shore with their phone numbers written on sheets. As Reg Myers remembers, "The Australian men were off fighting somewhere. About a month later when they came back, there were so many fights with the Americans that it was a relief for everybody when our ship was repaired enough to go back to sea."

This time, the ship headed to Bremerton, Washington, where she was fitted with a new bow. "We still had the same captain who had ordered us to abandon ship when we were hit by that torpedo."

Later, Myers was assigned to the USS *Minneapolis*. He became the commanding officer of the fifty Marines who manned the ship's guns. Because of this assignment, Myers became involved in every South Pacific island the Marines invaded between June 1942 and June 1944. Myers and his Marines assisted in a total of thirteen combat operations, including the invasions of Guadalcanal, Iwo Jima, and Okinawa.

By now, Myers himself was a captain. He stayed on the *Minneapolis* until the fall of 1944. Then he went to Okinawa, where preparations were being made to invade the main Japanese islands. These were expected to be the bloodiest battles in all of World War II. It was now March 1945.

The Army wanted to take the Japanese mainland with as few casualties as possible, but the Marines wanted to do it as fast as possible. The landing was going to occur close to Tokyo, with the hope that this would force the Japanese to surrender early. "Luckily, before this bloodbath could occur," says Myers, "the atomic bombs dropped on Hiroshima and Nagasaki ended the war and saved many thousands of American lives."

After the war, Myers was sent to China where he spent eight months as a logistics officer with the 5th Marine Regiment in

Peking (now called Beijing). Later he came back to the United States and was made the commanding officer of a Marine re-training command in Norfolk, Virginia. By 1950, Myers had been promoted to major. And talk of another conflict was starting.

In Korea, UN forces were being pushed back to the sea—to the "Pusan Perimeter." In answer to this threat, the Marine Corps re-formed a division to fight in Korea. Myers was sent first to Camp Pendleton in California, and then on to Japan in July 1950. He became the executive officer of one of the Marine battalions preparing to land at Inchon.

Myers remembers, "At Inchon, the tides were very large. If you hit them too low, you would land in deep mud and be exposed to enemy fire until you hit the beach." On landing, his battalion was in the lead. Being the executive officer of the battalion, Myers had his own LVT amphibious landing vehicle. Myers's commander ordered him to land on the southern flank of the battalion and report about any resistance he encountered. There was very little.

After landing, Myers's battalion advanced up a road against casual firing. They went into Seoul, where they spent two to three days cleaning up any remaining pockets of enemy soldiers. It was clear that, as the Americans were making their way from Seoul to the thirty-second parallel, the North Koreans were falling back pretty quickly. "The artillery was doing a pretty good job on the enemy, and the North Koreans weren't that well organized or led," remembers Myers. His battalion continued to lead the offensive northward.

When they got to the thirty-second parallel, General Douglas MacArthur then had to make the decision whether to go into North Korea. The big question of the day became, "Are the Chinese going to help the North Koreans?"

The North Koreans were leaderless and were falling apart, and the Americans wanted to block the Chinese from coming over the Yalu River to help the North Koreans. The Americans also wanted to block the North Koreans from using China as a safe haven. What they didn't know was that the Chinese were already in North Korea.

When General MacArthur had decided on a plan, the U.S. Army 10th Corps and the 1st Marine Division pulled back from the thirty-second parallel and made a landing at Hung Nam, deep in North Korea. This landing force then swept west with the intention of cutting off any North Korean retreat. About fifteen miles due west of the landing site, the Marines came to a six-thousand-foot plateau. About ten miles farther west was Hagaru-ri, and just north of this was the Chosin Reservoir. To the west was the twenty-five-mile road from China into North Korea where the infamous, erratic 10th Corps Army withdrawal eventually occurred, later described in S. L. A. Marshall's book *The River and the Gauntlet*. It was during this withdrawal that soldiers were told, "It's every man for himself"—an order that resulted in men being trampled in a wild retreat.

The Yalu River separates North Korea and China. The Marines and the Army were ordered to seize two critical bridges over this river, in order to block the Chinese from helping the North Koreans and to keep North Koreans from escaping into China.

The 5th and 7th Marine regiments went up to the Yalu from Hagaru-ri. Myers stayed with two companies at Hagaru-ri to secure this potentially important escape route if the need should arise. As it turned out, the need did arise.

"We had Marines and Army troops ahead of us at the Yalu River," remembers Myers. "Another company, commanded by the future Medal of Honor recipient Carl Sitter, was defending the plateau to the east of us."

When Myers and his battalion arrived at Hagaru-ri on November 26, 1950, it was minus twenty-five degrees Fahrenheit. The ground was so hard, the men couldn't use shovels to dig their foxholes, so they used dynamite. It was Sunday, and Myers's battalion commander, Colonel Tommie Ridge, was the only infantry commander at Hagaru-ri. Colonel Ridge used Korean intelligence agents to get information about the surrounding area. These agents were highly capable individuals, and they did their jobs well.

On Monday morning, the Korean agents came back from an area recon and told Tommie Ridge that the Chinese were going to hit Hagaru-ri that night at 7 p.m. The question was, if this was true, how did the Chinese get through the Marine and Army soldiers guarding the Yalu River? Could they have already been there? Or were they getting around the guards at the river? Colonel Ridge went to the commanding general of the Marine division, and to the G-3 with him, and told them about his report.

After hearing the story, the G-3 said, "I don't believe this." Colonel Ridge did believe it, and he tried to convince the general, saying, "General, you have nothing to lose. If it's not true, our preparations will have just been an exercise. But if it is true and we aren't prepared, we could lose the war."

The colonel was right and the G-3 gave in, even though his staff still didn't think anything needed to be done. The general put Colonel Ridge in command of the Hagaru-ri "defenses," which consisted of only two rifle companies and some reservists. With these few men and anyone else who could possibly act as a rifleman, the colonel and Myers established the perimeter of defense.

Above Hagaru-ri to the north were two hills held by future Medal of Honor recipient Bill Barber. These two hills straddled the road that the Marines and Army troops at the Yalu River would have to travel in the event of a withdrawal. This rear action led by Barber was necessary to keep the Marine and Army main forces guarding the bridges from becoming surrounded and trapped.

The perimeter of defense around Hagaru-ri consisted of about two thousand men. Of these, about five hundred were legitimate soldiers, while the rest were "candlestick makers and cooks." They were support troops, not combat soldiers.

At 7 p.m. Monday night, the colonel said to Myers, "Maybe I was wrong: the Chinese aren't attacking like intelligence reported they would." But at 9 p.m., the enemy attacked with a vengeance. Colonel Ridge had been right, after all.

Chinese attacking forces tried to come between the two rifle units planted on Hagaru-ri's southern flank. This defensive position held. The defense battalion's one reserve rifle platoon was called forward, and the Chinese were driven back. But all Monday night, the Chinese continued their attacks, trying to gain control of the two southern hills below Hagaru-ri.

Just northeast of Hagaru-ri were elements of the U.S. Army's 10th Corps Headquarters. A hill overlooking this headquarters, called East Hill, had Army troops assigned to hold it. This had become a very important assignment: by the early morning hours of Tuesday, November 28, 1950, a fierce Chinese assault on the hill began. Having had no success in the area south of Hagaru-ri, additional Chinese units were now available for this attack in the northeast.

Because the Army was holding East Hill, during the night Colonel Ridge sent a Marine corporal who was a radio operator up the hill to broadcast status reports. The hill was about one thousand feet high, covered with snow about eight to ten inches deep.

By early morning, the Chinese attack on East Hill was succeeding. First, Colonel Ridge lost communication with the Army colonel in charge of East Hill. Then, the Marine Command in Hagaru-ri started hearing whispers over the radio from the Marine corporal, who said he was surrounded by Chinese. It turned out that he had been left behind by the Army when they withdrew: the Army colonel in charge of the hill left so quickly, the Marine radio man was not even told about the retreat. Thus, the Marine was now left on the hill alone.

Colonel Ridge sent some Marines to the base of East Hill to see what was happening. They saw Army troops milling around without leadership. Their Army colonel had evacuated the area to report directly to his commander.

By 5 p.m. Tuesday, Colonel Ridge ordered Major Myers to take command of the Army typists, candlestick makers, and whatever Marines he could find, and retake East Hill. His exact words were, "Pick up any Marines you see standing on the road and go to East Hill." Myers was able to find about 150 Army soldiers and 15 Marines. When he arrived at the bottom of East Hill, Myers found two Marine tanks there. He ordered them to aim their guns at the Army troops to keep them from running away. Again, these men—except for the Marines—were not trained as combat soldiers.

"I was now at company strength and I hastily formed three platoons with a Marine lieutenant in charge of each group," remembers Myers. "By 2000 hours on Tuesday evening, we were ready for attack. I ordered the three platoons to begin moving up the southwest side of East Hill."

It was very cold when the combined Army and Marine company started up the hill. About a third of the way up, bullets began cracking into the frozen ground, causing an eerie sound in the cold atmosphere. When the first bullets started, some of the soldiers hit the ground and stopped their advance. "On the ground you move very little, and I couldn't get them back to their feet to continue the attack," remembers Myers. He started going from man to man and group to group, kicking their feet and yelling for them to go forward.

Finally, Myers pulled out his revolver and gave the men two choices: either get up or they would be shot. "I wouldn't have really shot anyone, but they didn't know me and they thought I just might," remembers Myers. "The most I would have done would be to fire in a soldier's vicinity if he didn't get up." The strategy worked, in any case, because the soldiers started getting up and moving forward again. "I was a Marine Corps major with a job and a responsibility," says Myers. "I intended to do my job."

The men continued going forward, firing their weapons as they went, and the Chinese started to fall back from the top of the hill. Marine artillery shells were finding their marks. The men continued the advance and finally came across the foxhole where the Marine corporal had been hiding. He became Myers's radio operator.

"We made our way up to the hilltop," Myers remembers. "The Chinese resistance was now decreasing except for artillery shells. By now, we had quite a few wounded men." Myers noticed that every time someone got wounded, though, about four of the Army guys would leave the battle to take the wounded soldier down the hill. "It seemed like we lost about five guys for every one who was wounded," observed Myers. "The Army guys seemed to be looking for any reason they could find to get out of there." Myers finally called down to head-quarters and told them to force the exiting soldiers back up the hill to join the battle. The troops who were not regular combat soldiers were showing their lack of discipline.

When Myers and his remaining troops finally secured the top of the hill, they set a defensive position for the night. The Chinese had set up "grazing" machine guns at the top of another hill, just north of the Americans. The Chinese started lobbing grenades and counterattacking the east side of East Hill.

All night long, white phosphorus grenades were going off. No one got any sleep. It was bitter cold. Troops on both sides yelled and screamed at each other. Constant machine-gun fire and the occasional explosion of a hand grenade completed the orgy of sound. By sunrise, Myers had only about 175 troops left. Many more of his undisciplined troops had left the top of the hill during the night.

"These Army guys weren't combat soldiers," stresses Myers. "They were administrative personnel who didn't know me and I didn't know them. We had very few officers in the group. Frankly, I couldn't have expected much from them. My Marines stayed with me, but there weren't enough of them."

Because of the grazing machine-gun fire, the Chinese had the Americans pinned down throughout the day on Wednesday. Myers's radio operator—the Marine corporal—was shot through the back, and Myers knew they wouldn't be able to hold this hill much longer.

He reported his dilemma to Colonel Ridge, who—with his own limited number of men—had all he could do to keep the rest of the Hagaru-ri defenses in place. Ridge called Colonel

Chesty Puller at Koto-ri on the east road to the ocean, and asked Puller if he could send help to the headquarters area.

Puller sent a Marine rifle company led by Captain Carl Sitter, along with a Multinational Task Force unit consisting of British marines. As these reinforcements started west on the road to Hagaru-ri, they ran into intense enemy fire that forced the Multinational Task Force to withdraw. But Captain Sitter refused to pull back: his company continued fighting forward. Colonel Puller radioed the brave captain—who would soon earn his own Medal of Honor—and said, "Get at 'em, buddy." Sitter did; and when he got to the Hagaru-ri area, Colonel Ridge ordered him to relieve Myers on East Hill.

"When Sitter and his company made it to the top of the hill to relieve me, I was never so happy to see someone in my life," recalls Myers. "He had battle-experienced Marines with him, who were real fighting men. I thanked God when those three rifle platoons with full radio communications took over." By then, most of Myers's Army "company" was gone. His Marines were still with him.

Myers and his tired men went down to the headquarters area for rest.

On Thursday, when the 5th and 7th Marines came down the road into Hagaru-ri from the Yalu River area, they marched parade straight and started singing the Marine Corps hymn. They knew they were marching through an area that had been kept clear for them by a small group of brave men at a very large price. Every Marine and soldier from those platoons who had sacrificed so much during the previous three days stood at attention, knowing they were being thanked. Their pride was real.

Later, as the Marines were withdrawing along the east road from their headquarters position, they started coming across abandoned Army vehicles. The Marines took them, eventually painting over the Army insignia and replacing them with Marine markings. Back in South Korea, then, the Marines had no shortage of transportation—that is, until an Army general got wind of what happened. He ordered the Marines to give back the vehicles the Army had abandoned in North Korea.

Myers received his orders to go home in April 1951. A mortar shell had fallen next to him, and he was wounded. First he was sent to Japan and then back to the United States. The war was over for Myers.

"I have a very strong loyalty to the Marine Corps," says Myers. "The esprit de corps of a Marine is dominating. Every man who was once a Marine understands the saying 'Once a Marine, always a Marine.' "

Congressional Medal of Honor recipient Reginald Myers is certainly a Marine.

8.

JOHN F. BAKER, JR.

Standing Tall

Some men approach their jobs with incredible enthusiasm and aggressiveness. In baseball, Pete Rose was called "Mr. Hustle" because everything he did was full out. During World War II, General George Patton's tanks were often way ahead of everyone else in their drive to Germany. These men seemed to have higher expectations for themselves than other people did.

During the Vietnam War, John Baker was one soldier who also had higher expectations for himself. "Gung ho" might be a way to describe it. But it was this enthusiasm to the job at hand that caused this Medal of Honor recipient to step forward when the time came, and to do the job above and beyond what was expected of him.

John F. Baker, Jr.
Private First Class, U.S. Army
Republic of Vietnam
5 November 1966

Standing only five foot two, John Baker might be considered a short man. The Navy and the Marines considered him that. They wouldn't even let him enlist when he graduated from his Moline, Illinois, high school. They said he was too short. So, on January 10, 1966, Baker joined the Army. The Army soon found out that height had nothing to do with how tall this man could be.

John Baker was in good shape, and he immediately liked his new life. He remembers, "I decided to join the military because I wanted to travel and see the world. I guess you could say I was a 'gung ho' soldier."

Baker took the nickname *Short Round* in good spirits. He went first to artillery training and then to airborne school at Fort Benning, Georgia. Vietnam was his next destination. On August 5, 1966, he found himself in the middle of a war. Initially stationed with the 25th Infantry Division and attached to the 3rd of 13th Artillery Group, he loaded rounds into self-propelled howitzers. This wasn't a dangerous job. In fact, for a soldier who wanted to see action, it was actually quite boring.

After a month of loading rounds, Baker decided he was ready for combat. He transferred to the "Wolfhounds" of the 25th Infantry. He knew this was a famous division, but he didn't know he would soon be adding to its military lore.

"My job was assistant machine gunner," Baker remembers. "I carried the ammunition for an M-60 machine gun while our platoon was on patrol. I usually carried four belts of ammunition with a hundred rounds per belt. Our machine gun could use a belt in thirty seconds!"

Baker loved the Wolfhounds. The troops were working Hell's Half Acres and Boliel's Woods. They would helicopter or trek out each evening and set up night ambushes for Vietcong coming in from Cambodia. The patrols were made up of a reinforced platoon consisting of thirty-six men and two M-60 machine guns. "We would reach our objective about 1 a.m. and set up our perimeter for the Vietcong ambush," Baker recalls. "About every other night, we would kill two to five Vietcong. We would also have one or more of our guys get killed or wounded. In fact, quite a few of our men were eventually killed."

Baker, at twenty years old, was a little older than the rest of the men. He remembers, "I had a job to do. But as a soldier, my biggest job was to help my fellow soldier. We looked out for each other." As Baker became more experienced, he became more cautious. Ambushing was a dangerous business where experience counted a lot. He started getting good at it. In fact, within his company he started getting a reputation as a daredevil. Baker remembers how these patrols would give him an adrenaline rush, but he also remembers how he started to become scared of dying. "Anyone who tells you they weren't scared of dying in combat isn't telling the truth," Baker says.

On these early missions, and because of his size and aggressiveness, Baker learned another skill: that of the tunnel rat. "I volunteered for this job because I'm only five foot two," Baker recalls. "There were a couple days training, but most of the training was on the job. You learned how to be careful in the tunnels. You learned how to find the 'punching pits,' which were holes with trap doors opening into pungi sticks. You also learned how to avoid the 'two step' snakes. These were the ones which bit you, giving you two steps before you were dead. We became experts in booby traps which the enemy liked to leave for us."

The tunnel missions consisted of three men. Baker was always in the second position of the three men because he was the radio and "pace" man. His job was to radio continuously up to the platoon leader and tell him how many paces the team had walked and in what direction. The rest of the platoon would pace along above the ground, following the tunnel team so they could immediately start digging in case the tunnel caved in. "I went into over a hundred tunnels during my year in Vietnam, and I found myself in a tunnel combat situation about eight times," Baker recalls. "After my first time through a tunnel, I decided I liked that kind of excitement."

The worst job of a tunnel rat was when he found bodies of enemy soldiers who had died. The enemy would bury their dead in the back of their tunnels. The tunnel rats had to dig these dead soldiers out and drag them up, so it could be determined how they died. "The type of wound was evidently important for someone to know," Baker recalls. "Some of those bodies were decayed and they really smelled. It would make you feel sick."

The biggest tunnel Baker ever found was near the Cambodian border. A tank had caused a small collapse in the ground, and the soldiers knew something must be down there. As it turned out, the tunnel was built during the French War in the 1950s. It had three levels. The first level was down fifty feet from the surface—much deeper than the usual fifteen to twenty feet. And this particular tunnel still served as a big hospital. It had beds, electric generators, and even blood in the refrigerators. Evidently, the enemy had known that the American troops were coming, and got out of there.

Baker remembers the fear he felt from being in such a large tunnel. "The rooms were big—as big as living rooms in a house—and they were all cemented in. We found documents and ammunition down there, and then we set dynamite charges to blow it up. We got out of there pretty quickly. We were happy to still be alive."

A tunnel rat had a very dangerous job. It was always dark, and you never knew who or what you would run into. It was in a tunnel that Baker earned a Purple Heart in February 1967. He remembers, "I was with two other guys about a quarter mile inside a tunnel. We came around a bend, and a Vietcong was there waiting for us. When he saw us, he threw a grenade. The guy directly in front of me lost his life in the explosion. Shrapnel flew into me, but I immediately zapped the Vietcong. I lost a good friend that day. He had been through basic training with me. And through quite a few tunnels. I could have easily died too."

By October 30, 1966, Baker had been in country for about two months. The base had sent an eight-man patrol out the night before, and it never came back. The next morning, Baker's thirty-six-man platoon was ordered to go out and find the missing men.

They finally found them about fifty miles from the base. The soldiers had been caught by the enemy and told to take their clothes off. Then, one by one, they were hacked up with a machete and executed with a bullet to the head. Baker's platoon called in helicopters to bring the bodies back to the base.

After the choppers left, Baker and his platoon began searching for Vietcong. They started through a sugar plantation and, after passing through a paddy, they started to receive fire from the rear. The Vietcong had buried themselves in the mud; the Americans had walked right over them. Some of the men in Baker's platoon, and a lot of the Vietcong, were killed in that firefight.

The platoon kept going forward another five miles before setting up a base camp for the night. By this time, the original search platoon had been joined by the entire company of two hundred men. The commanders had decided that this was too much contact: the enemy must have something going on. But the men just sat there for several days, waiting for more Vietcong to come through from Cambodia. None came.

After the company finally left to go back to their base, the men heard that a regiment of hard-core North Vietnamese "regulars" had come through looking for them. There had been more than a thousand enemy soldiers ready to annihilate the Americans. And with those numbers, they probably would have.

Baker's next night patrol was on November 5, 1966. Another company's recon patrol had been trapped by the enemy. The Americans knew generally where the patrol was, and Baker and his company were sent out to get them.

The trapped patrol consisted of eight men who had gone out near a Special Forces camp at Virgin Mountain. They were trapped by an unknown number of enemy troops. Baker's company flew into the area during the late afternoon and had planned on going after the trapped squad the next morning. It started getting dark. The Americans began hearing sounds in the surrounding jungle. At first, the sounds were unclear. Then they were identified as laughter, which got louder and louder. Pretty soon the Vietcong were taunting the Americans, telling them they better go home. The laughter of the Vietcong kept up all night long.

The next morning, the company commander—Captain Robert Foley—ordered his men into the jungle. The men went from bright daylight to darkness in seconds as they walked into the thick jungle growth. All of a sudden, about fifty feet in, enemy fire started coming from everywhere. It came from the sides, the front, and above the surrounded Americans. As Baker remembers, "Everyone was getting shot. The radio operator was shot. And we all hit the ground, firing back. There were snipers above us, and we shot them immediately."

Captain Foley asked for two volunteers to crawl ahead and give a report on the enemy. The medic and another soldier took their gear off and started crawling forward. The enemy fire became less intense as the two volunteers made their way up. Then, about twenty-five yards in, the fire increased again, killing the soldier and wounding the medic. He started screaming, but the enemy wouldn't finish him off.

Meanwhile, more Vietcong snipers had tied themselves into the trees above the Americans; they started firing. "They were all over," Baker remembers. Captain Foley ordered Baker forward. Baker took his gear off and crawled to within five feet of the wounded medic. He couldn't get any closer. He could see that the downed soldier was full of bullet holes and suffering. The Vietnamese were letting him scream so the other Americans would come into their killing zone. Baker could also see some

L-shaped cement bunkers with enemy machine gunners just beyond the downed medic. Baker crawled back and told his commander.

Captain Foley gave the command for the entire company to move forward. The Americans started getting hit again. Baker's machine gunner was struck in the arm, and the impact ripped his hand off. Grabbing the machine gunner, Baker dragged him to the rear. Then he picked up some more ammunition and worked his way to the front again. With the machine gun now his, Baker killed six snipers in the trees.

By now, he was the forward soldier in the company; he could see that the medic was still alive. The rest of the men were pinned down, but some of the soldiers were trying to get forward. Guns were firing everywhere, and Americans were being shot.

Baker kept crawling forward—toward the three enemy bunkers that were killing the Americans. When he got close, he put his machine gun down and lobbed a grenade into the first bunker, getting a direct hit. Two Vietcong were killed. Quickly—before he was seen—he started crawling toward the second bunker and threw another grenade, killing two more enemy soldiers. Toward the third bunker he threw another grenade, this time killing three more enemy machine gunners.

Baker's actions caused him to become the primary target of the tree snipers, who were now trying desperately to stop him. Bullets started cracking everywhere, and Baker started firing up. Incredibly, he killed three before his gun ran out of ammunition. Making his way back to the American line for more ammo, he realized that Captain Foley had repositioned the company attack to the left side. There were now many wounded Americans in the jungle, and Baker started back in, pulling as many as he could to the rear. Snipers continued shooting from the trees. Baker killed three more.

Baker remembers an American soldier who passed by him while running frantically toward the rear. Baker looked up and saw the terror in this soldier's face just as a .50-caliber machine gun blasted his head. "It blew wide open," Baker recalls. "At that point, something inside me took over. My adrenaline was flowing and I went on 'automatic' with more strength and power than I'd ever had."

Baker stood up with his machine gun and started running into the enemy fire. Shooting wildly, he charged into the remaining enemy bunkers. "I don't remember many details of this, but they say I knocked out six more bunkers and killed fifty or sixty more enemy soldiers. I remember hearing bullets fly by as I charged forward. Some of those bullets were so close to me, I could feel them pass."

A grenade exploded in front of Baker, throwing him off his feet. He stood back up and continued his one-man charge into the bunkers. His machine gun was tearing into the enemy. The rest of the company started following him in. The enemy was being routed.

The eight trapped soldiers could now see the Americans, and they made a dash toward them. Baker remembers, "They were pretty shot up, but they were also pretty glad to see us."

The battle was over for Baker's company, but it was just beginning for everyone else. Three thousand enemy troops were either in the area or on the way. By the time Baker and his company returned to their perimeter, B-52 bombers were already scourging the area and helicopters were everywhere, bringing in American troops. The 1st Infantry Division ("Big Red One"), the Marines, and the rest of the 25th Infantry Division were coming in. This became Operation Attleboro—one of the largest American offensives during the Vietnam War. Baker and his company had been the beginning of it.

Later that day, Baker and the other men were choppered out to the base of Virgin Mountain. Baker's whole uniform was covered with blood and mud. The men stayed there for a couple of days. Baker had to be told what he had accomplished. "I really didn't remember much," says Baker. "I was pretty scared for a couple days after they told me this stuff. My hands shook constantly. I should have been killed." Of the 257 men in the company, one in four was either killed or wounded. By the time the entire offensive was over, twenty-two hundred enemy soldiers had been killed.

Baker remembers, "I was out of control. Anger and fear were my most prevalent emotions. It's something to see a fellow soldier killed right in front of you. Something flexes and breaks in your mind. You feel rage. It's not pleasurable. You're scared to death, but you start killing back."

On Baker's last day in Vietnam on August 5, 1967, he was told about his recommendation for the Congressional Medal of Honor. News of his his recommendation was picked up by a local newspaper in Moline, Illinois. By the time Baker got home, people were talking about it. But another local newspaper couldn't get confirmation from the Pentagon, and reported this inability to confirm. Unfortunately, this made Baker look foolish. His family started getting anonymous phone calls; people would laugh and talk about "faker Baker." Rather than have his family experience this humiliation, Baker decided to cut short his home leave, and get out of town. It was a pretty embarrassing time for this person who was to become the town's greatest hero.

In October 1968, President Lyndon Johnson called and told Baker he would indeed receive the medal in two weeks. And so, on November 3, 1968, President Johnson presented the Medal of Honor to John Baker. The scoffers in Moline were now silent. And the town even built him a house.

Baker remained in the Army for twenty-four years, retiring in November 1989. As he says, "My Army time was a good experience. I miss the friendship and the camaraderie. I wear a Medal of Honor because of the men I served with. A lot of brave people performed the same actions I did. I wear my medal out of respect for those men who died in actions not seen, and therefore not remembered."

These men Baker speaks of are unseen heroes honored now by a man tall enough to reach them, by a man whose height cannot be measured in inches.

9.

LEWIS L. MILLETT

Freedom's Warrior

The United States has fought wars throughout its history, beginning with the American Revolution. Family military traditions have sometimes influenced the participants in these wars.

The Millett family has such a tradition. When Lewis Millett received his Medal of Honor, the award was consistent with his family history. It's expected that a Millett will participate when needed in battle for his country. Every Millett understands this. It's the way it's always been.

Lewis L. Millett
Captain, U.S. Army
Vicinity of Soam-ni, Korea
7 February 1951

Thomas Millett came to the Massachusetts Bay Colony in 1635 and was killed at the Brookfield Indian Massacre in 1675. His son, John Millett, fought with the Gloucester Regiment during the American Revolution. Both of Lewis Millet's grandfathers fought in the Civil War. A great uncle, William Millett, is buried at the infamous prison compound in Andersonville, Georgia.

In fact, a Millett has fought in every U.S. war from the very beginning. The Milletts have continued to pay more than their share of freedom's price, including their most recent payment when Sergeant John Morton Millett and 246 other soldiers from the 101st Sinai Task Force died on December 12, 1985.

Lewis Millett was born in Mechanic Falls, Maine—about thirty-five miles from Portland—on December 15, 1920. He went to high school while Hitler was building his power in Germany and Japan was expanding its empire in Asia. After graduation, Millett volunteered to go into the Marine Corps, but he was told he would have to wait a couple of weeks for a physical exam. Young, impatient, and ready to fight, Millett didn't want to wait, so he joined the Army instead. It was 1940.

First it was basic training in Fort Devins, Massachusetts; then to air gunnery and armory school. Millett was now a private first class making thirty-six dollars per month. "We didn't have real guns so we practiced with broomsticks," says Millett.

In October 1941, President Franklin Delano Roosevelt was saying that America wasn't going to fight. Millett could see that Canada was, so he decided that Canada was where he wanted to be. He crossed the border in Maine and went to a Canadian Army recruiter. When the recruiter asked, "Where are you from?" Millett told him Maine. The recruiter said, "No problem. Ontario is a nice place to be from. Welcome to the Canadian Army."

It was November 1941. Millett was not only in the Canadian Army; he was also AWOL from the U.S. Army. But Millett was going to fight. "I went through basic training again, this time at Evanston, New Brunswick."

When Pearl Harbor was attacked, Millett was sent to London where he went through the British Army Commando School. Millett was told that any American who wanted to could transfer into the U.S. Army. "I transfered back," Millett remembers. "I hadn't thought much about deserting the American Army to join the Canadian Army."

Millett was transferred to the U.S. 1st Armored Division— "Old Ironsides." He trained in England and then Scotland, before shipping off for the landing in North Africa. It was November 1942.

By now, Lewis Millett was a proud commando-trained soldier. A tall steel-faced young man sporting a long reddish handlebar mustache at a time long before (and after) such things were popular, he was more than ready to go to battle. In his fatigues, holding his rifle with hand grenades strung around his neck, he looked like the warrior he was.

Millett went ashore in Algeria on the beach at Saint Leu near the Oran harbor. The landing was easy with little resistance. The American objective was to take Tunis, alongside the English. "We got within a few miles of Tunis and got into a knock-down, drag-out fight with German Panzer tanks of the Afrika Korps," remembers Millett. "I was part of Baker Battery. We had a camouflaged wheat haystack where we hid our thirty-seven-millimeter antitank gun." Some American tanks came through the position and fired a round through the haystack. Millett started yelling, "Cease fire! Cease fire!" The American tanks saw the Americans and stopped their fire. Then they started to cross the valley toward a slowly rising ridge line.

"Only one of those twenty tanks made it. They were annihilated by the German 88s. Then the Germans came back at us with their tanks."

Millett was manning an antitank gun. He got off about five rounds, which hit an enemy tank. "I watched my shells bounce right off that tank's sides," remembers Millett. "When the driver noticed me, he shot back a short uninspired machine-gun blast—sort of like, 'Thanks, but don't bother.' That's a little discouraging."

The Germans started firing at the Americans with a vengeance. The haystack caught fire. Two American half-tracks filled with ammunition were hidden in the burning haystack, and Millett knew they were about to blow. He raced through the artillery barrage and got to them just in time to retrieve them. Millett received his first combat medal—a Bronze Star—for this action.

By now, Baker Battery was firing artillery north, south, east, and west. It didn't take a genius to figure out the Americans were surrounded. "That's a numbing shock," Millett remembers. "We didn't know how we were going to get out of this mess."

The men of Baker Battery fired until they were out of ammunition. They tried to pull back toward the rock-covered hills. Millett drove the last half-track of the battalion's withdrawal. The men drove all night to escape the Germans.

Finally, the battalion pulled into a big valley. "If the Germans had continued attacking, they could have knocked us off," says Millett. "There were literally thousands of us in a wide open valley. The Stuks JU87s could have come at us then, and reamed us."

Later, at the bloody Kasserine Pass, Millett shot down a Messerschmitt 109 with his twin 50s. The plane had been strafing the troops. But Millett fired at him without permission. He was promoted to corporal, but he also got chewed out for shooting without permission. "We were on a hillside overlooking a valley filled with Germans," remembers Millett. "We were dug in and camouflaged. We could see German tanks below us. I guess I gave away our position when I shot that plane."

Millett fought throughout North Africa for six months until the famous German Afrika Korps were finally bottled up in Bizerte and Tunis.

After Africa, Millett went to Salerno, Italy. He was now a buck sergeant. He volunteered to become a forward observer, directing the artillery that supports the infantry. Because a forward observer is up front with the infantry, the job taught Millett how to be an infantryman. He worked in this slot throughout the Italian campaign.

Because the terrain would not allow it, very little armor could be used in Italy. The forward observer teams were especially important for calling in long-range artillery support that the tanks could not provide. Each team consisted of three to six men with a jeep and a half-track.

"I provided forward observer support for all the major units in Italy," remembers Millett. "We even supported the 'Devil's Brigade.' "

In Naples—almost two years later—the U.S. Army finally caught up with Millett. He was court-martialed for his desertion two years before when he joined the Canadian Army. Three times, his commander was told to court-martial him. But it wasn't until the third time that the commander was *ordered* to. Millett was found guilty, fined, and sentenced to thirty days of hard labor. He paid the thirty-dollar fine, but his commander figured that thirty days of hard labor was adequately served as a forward observer. Millett had paid his price for desertion.

One time, on patrol for the infantry, Millett had with him a lieutenant who just wanted to fire the guns and say they had completed their mission and go back. This eight-man patrol had Italian partisans and infantry with them. "So we fired our guns, and the lieutenant started to go back," remembers Millett. "I said, 'To hell with this. I'm not leaving because we haven't gotten the enemy troop information yet.' About three of the guerillas decided to stay with me. The other guys left."

Later, the new and smaller patrol ran into enemy troops with machine guns. The Americans captured a prisoner. They interrogated him and brought him back so even more information could be obtained. Millett was promoted to lieutenant. His commander called him in and said, "Millett, stop doing these crazy things."

Later, the call went out for Airborne volunteers. Many men had been lost jumping into the mountains, and more people were now needed. Millett saw the call as a ticket to more action, and so he volunteered. But he was turned down. He asked his commander why and was told, "Millett, you're damned good. But you get into too many fights in the rear." Millett did love a good fight—preferably, but not necessarily, with the enemy.

Later, Millett was working as a forward observer in a battle up in the north, in the Appians. GIs were attacking the Chinquale Canal, near a town above Rome on the edge of Apennines. Millett was forward-supporting a unit of all-black enlisted men. The unit became surrounded in enemy territory. The Germans unleashed a massive attack that seemed certain to overrun the U.S. infantry. Many troops ran, and it looked like those staying were going to be overrun. Realizing the danger, Millett called artillery fire down on his own position and drove the Germans back. His action allowed the remaining soldiers to withdraw. Millett got another Bronze Star.

By May 1945, the war had ended. The military had more men than it needed, so Millett was discharged.

Millett's mother wanted to see her son again. He had been writing her throughout the war, telling her he was a logistics clerk—way out of the action—and wishing he could get into combat. He didn't want his mother to worry. "Well, when I got home, I found out my mother had been receiving military copies of my combat medals all along," Millett recalls. "My mother's hair had turned completely white." Millett knew why.

Millett transferred into the National Guard and entered Bates College in Portland, Maine. By 1948, the military began requesting volunteers, anticipating a possible conflict in Korea.

Millett signed up for active duty. He would have graduated from college in June 1949. Instead, he was called up in January 1949.

The Americans were down to bare bones, militarily, when the Korean War broke out. Millett was sent to Japan and told he would be an artillery officer. He was assigned artillery support to the elite 27th "Wolfhound" Regiment of the 25th Division. Normally, a regiment has three battalions. But at the beginning of the Korean War, the 27th had only two battalions, and even those two were undermanned. When war broke out, however, the 27th Regiment was sent to Korea.

Millett's artillery unit was stationed near the Pusan Perimeter in a location that regularly saw the enemy break through the lines. Millett led a reinforced commando platoon that protected his gun positions. He trained this special unit of fifty men to protect the gun emplacement perimeters at night. The artillery were favorite targets of the enemy, especially early in the war when the Americans were undermanned, and the Chinese could do just about anything they wanted.

Brigadier General George B. Barth, artillery commander of the division, later remarked, "I am convinced Millett doesn't know what it means to be afraid. I know of no other man in whose behalf I can make such an unequivocal statement."

Part of Millett's commando unit was made up of bad kids. "They were the type their superiors didn't know whether to give medals to or throw in the stockade," Millett remembers. "I ran their fannies off. There was lots of PT and lots of discipline."

At the end of July 1950, the Americans experienced six of the most grueling days and one of the toughest fights of the Korean War. Millett's 8th Field Artillery was supporting the 27th Infantry Wolfhounds at Hwanggang-ni. It was a time when steadiness of leadership could tip the scales of victory or defeat.

The important question for General Barth was whether his artillery units would continue to fire their guns while receiving fire from the enemy. He received his answer early on, when he heard about Lieutenant Millett in action.

A unit started receiving fire and Millett picked up a piece of clay pottery, began tapping it, and marched through the battery's gunners while singing a variation of a Salvation Army street song: "Come on, you drunken bums. Put a nickel on the drum. Put a nickel on the drum and pull the lanyard on your guns, and you'll be saved! Now, get on your guns and start firing!"

The effect was electric. The men, grinning and amazed, manned their 105 tubes and started firing. Even though they were taking casualties from the enemy fire, they didn't stop serving their pieces until the enemy had had enough. Inspired by the courage of this unknown lieutenant, the 8th Field Artillery had met the supreme test of good artillery: counterfiring while under fire.

"I didn't know that anyone was watching, but evidently the artillery officer in charge saw what I did and told the general about this crazy guy who sang to the guys under fire," Millett remembers.

One night, the enemy came through the American line between Fox Company on one hill and Easy Company and George Company on another. American tanks were supposedly on the road, protecting the approaches; but a large number of Chinese got through.

Millett was back at a command area with his men. "Most of us were lying on the ground resting," remembers Millett. "I heard a whole bunch of troops coming and I figured they had to be ours, this far back of the line. But they weren't. It was a whole damn battalion of enemy soldiers." The Chinese were marching past Millett's tent in double time only two hundred yards away. The enemy liked to break through a line and get to the rear as fast as they could before they started fighting.

Most of the GIs were still sleeping. Millett realized what was going on and started to get up. Somebody put a knee on Millett's stomach and put a hand over his mouth. "It was my sergeant, making sure that I didn't draw their attention," Millett remembers. "The Chinese kept running by us."

Millett always carried a belt with three grenades on either side. With these and his M-1 rifle, he slowly walked out of his tent, and nonchalantly fell in behind the enemy battalion. He started marching double time with them through the still sleeping U.S. troops. "Ambush and death was on my mind," he remembers.

Millett grabbed his grenades and threw all six forward as quickly as he could. He emptied his automatic rifle at everyone he could see, as the enemy troops started to scatter in confusion. Diving into a truck next to him, Millett mounted the truck's phosphorus gun and started firing. The phosphorus lit up the area. "I was shooting the hell out of these people and having a ball," remembers Millett. The Chinese took off up a ridge.

Millett looked around, expecting to see other guys shooting. There wasn't a single guy around. He was alone. He called out for his commander: "Hey, Colonel Burch, where are you?"

Millett received only a Bronze Medal for this action. But he found out why in a conversation he had with a soldier from Fox Company the next day. Evidently, when the Chinese battalion escaped up the ridge, they ran smack into and through a platoon from George Company, killing the entire platoon.

Thirty to forty enemy soldiers were killed by Millett's bold action. But, as he says, "I guess I made the infantry look bad. No one else took part. I was all alone."

Another time, Millett was ordered by his battalion commander to report to the command post. The commander, looking rather grim, told Millett that the American line at Sou Bak San was collapsing. He needed Millett to find another position for the artillery batteries in the area.

Millett started toward the front, accompanied by Easy Company. They began to see American troops—without weapons or gear—running toward them on the road. At first, it was just a few. Then large numbers of retreating troops started appearing. Millett and Easy Company were attacked. Easy Company had one tank, and it started firing the gun. Everybody else went down on the ground and began shooting their rifles. Retreating troops still kept passing Millett and his men.

The most difficult thing to do in combat is to retreat. "We were covering the withdrawal of an entire regiment and, by now, we had less than one hundred men," remembers Millett. "We stood our ground that night, and many fought to their deaths."

For the next several days, Millett's company continued to cover a hundred-mile withdrawal of American troops. It was miserably cold, and the troops were often in three to four feet of snow. The GIs drew to the rear from Osan and then back to Pyongtaek. The North Koreans were exerting tremendous pressure: they made no secret of the fact that they intended to drive the Americans into the sea.

After this withdrawal, the Americans held their position, waiting for the snow to pass. The time would come when the Americans—reorganized—would be ready to start fighting back north. In the meantime, a Chinese battle action report was intercepted, in which American tactics were described. It said the Americans didn't like close combat. "That was a bunch of bull," Millett recalls. The report drove Millett to make his men experts at the bayonet.

On November 27, 1950, Millett was with a task force at a forward observation post when he came under fire from enemy mortars. Shells started to burst near Millet. "I was standing outside my tent, calling in artillery, using the 'by guess and by god' method," Millett recalls. "A shell landed next to me and ripped my leg open with a fragment. All of a sudden, I was on the ground. When I stood up, I found my leg bleeding. I patched it up as well as I could." Just then, a trooper standing next to Millett was shot through the head. Millett picked up the fallen soldier's helmet and saw a picture of his wife and kids tucked inside it.

Later the call went out for wounded. The wounded were

placed on whatever could move them to the rear: ammo trucks, supply trucks, jeeps, and ambulances. Every wounded soldier was being sent to the rear. Millett consented to have his leg treated, but he refused to leave his rifle behind.

His refusal was a lifesaving decision. As they started back to the rear, the medical convoy was ambushed. Millett remembers, "We ran into a hellacious fire. I rolled out of the ambulance and into a ditch with a small group of men. We started moving directly into the enemy fire. If we had moved away from them— as they expected us to—we would have run either into their ambush killing zone or into their booby traps."

Millett, and the small group with him, crawled until they got beyond the enemy line of fire. They made their way to a perimeter held by Lieutenant Colonel Gordon E. Murch and the 2nd Battalion of the 27th Infantry. "I got to a radio and warned the guys in the back they were about to be hit," Millett recalls. "And they were, but at least they knew it was coming."

Millett loaded up again. His leg was bandaged and he could still walk, but just barely. He was put into a tank that had been hit earlier by an antitank grenade. The tank's front gunner had taken a direct hit. "The white paint inside that tank was covered with blood and human remains," remembers Millett. "The machine gun still worked though, and we had about fifteen boxes of ammo." The tank, with Millett manning one of the guns, started counterattacking toward the rear. It broke through, and Millett was taken to a MASH unit.

"People were moaning and suffering everywhere," Millett remembers. "I took my bandage off and I wasn't bleeding anymore. I figured these people were hurt worse than I was, so I left." He went back to his commander and was later assigned to be an air observer until his leg healed.

Millett began flying in a little L-4 Piper Cub. One day, flying near Panmunjom in the late afternoon, Millett and his pilot saw an American P-51 come over the mountain range and start circling them. The fighter let down his wheels and went over a ridge. They followed. The P-51 was trying to let the Piper spotter know that another P-51 was shot down.

Jim Lawrence was the pilot of the Piper. When he saw the downed P-51, he landed on a small dirt road next to it. Lawrence and Millett immediately located the downed pilot. He was a South African named John Davis. At first, Millett tried to get all three guys into the little airplane. But he couldn't do it. Then he told Lawrence to take off with the downed pilot and come back as soon as he could.

"I stayed on the ground and watched the Piper take off," Millett remembers. The downed P-51 was slowly discharging its guns, due to the heat of the crash. Every few minutes a short burst of ammunition would fire. Millett worried that the noise would give the position to the North Koreans in the area. And finally, sure enough, an enemy patrol started making its way toward the crash site.

As the enemy soldiers approached, they would duck every time the P-51 guns discharged, because they weren't sure if they were being fired upon or not. Cautiously, they made their way toward Millett. When their lead guy got close enough, Millett shot him through the forehead with his pistol. The rest of the enemy squad immediately scattered, thinking there were a number of Americans up there. Just then, Jim Lawrence and the Piper returned. Millett recalls, "I jumped on that little plane and we took off just as the North Koreans began attacking the crash site."

When Millett's leg wounds healed, he decided to volunteer for the infantry, so he went to Colonel Murch of the 27th Infantry Division and requested the transfer. Colonel Murch said he would love to have the aggressive young captain under his command. But Millett's own battalion commander made no secret of the fact that he thought Millett was an absolute raving maniac. The issue was decided by the artillery commander General Barth, who was a former infantryman himself. He told Millett, "Congratulations. Good luck to you and to Easy Company."

Millett transferred from the artillery to the infantry on January 1, 1951. His first job was the command of Easy Company of the 2nd Battalion's 27th Wolfhound Regiment. He was replacing

Captain Reginald Desiderio, who had been killed in the company's last action—the action in which Millett received his leg wound.

During that hellish night of battle, Easy Company had held against an overwhelming Chinese attack, constantly repeating to each other their captain's words: "Just hold until first light and we'll have it made." When Captain Desiderio was killed at the end of that long night, and the men had held, Easy Company's young executive officer crawled forward to his captain's lifeless body and—with tears in his eyes—told him, "Captain, it's first light, and we held on." Captain Desiderio received a Congressional Medal of Honor for his actions that night. These were pretty big shoes for Millett to fill.

"When I took over command of Easy Company, I decided my men were going to carry bayonets and know how to use them," remembers Millett. He hadn't forgotten the Chinese battle action report that had angered him several months before. Initially, Millett's company didn't have enough bayonets to go around, because few American soldiers actually carried them, let alone used them. So Millett scrounged. He scrounged until he found enough for everybody. Then the men trained. "We trained hard," Millett recalls. "We started to get pretty good—so good in fact, the men eventually practiced even during their breaks."

Other companies laughed at Easy Company. They thought bayonet practice was a waste of time. The people who knew Millett, however, knew he was serious. Millett was probably the best knife fighter and bayonet wielder in the U.S. Army, and he wanted his men to be like him.

"I was pleased with how well my men took to the bayonet," Millett recalls. "I gave the order that, from now on, the bayonets would be fixed when Easy Company attacked." Millett and his men were ready for a bayonet fight. Their fight was coming.

Operation Punch began during the early days of February 1951. The North Koreans had advanced as far as they would ever get. The U.S. 8th Army was at the limit of its recoil, awaiting orders to commence attack. The 27th Wolfhound Regiment of the 25th Infantry Division was scheduled to play a pivotal role in this attack, which would take the Americans from Suwon to the Han River.

Millett's company became part of the task force spearheading the attack north. The men followed a road regularly intersected by right-angle ridges all the way to the Han River. Accompanying the infantry were Pershing tanks from the 64th Tank Battalion.

On February 5, 1951, Millett and Easy Company started up the road through some low hills. They marched close together as they passed frozen rice paddies. Two tanks accompanied the infantry, with Fox Company on the left, and Millett's Easy Company on the right. Suddenly, Easy Company's 1st Platoon became pinned down by enemy fire as it approached a low ridge. A skirmish line was immediately set up. Automatic weapons fire started coming down into the GIs.

Millett—seeing the strength of the enemy position—yelled for 2nd Platoon to fix bayonets and move into the left flank of the pinned-down 1st Platoon. He ordered 3rd Platoon to cover the coming attack by firing their Browning Automatic rifles ("BARs"), machine guns, and M-1 rifles into the enemy ridge. Positioning himself at the base of the ridge with 1st and 2nd Platoons, Millett yelled, "Fix bayonets, men. Follow me!" With a fierce scream, he charged up the hill with his men following. Millett's wild screams were copied by his men as the Americans ran toward the surprised enemy. The Chinese guns were directed at the attackers.

The men of 3rd Platoon at the base of the hill—firing up at the hilltop—were surprised when all of a sudden they saw Millett appear on the ridge. He was holding his rifle in one hand and waving for his men to join him with the other. The communist forces streamed out of their foxholes and began retreating down the reverse slope. "We got close to the top of the hill, but they ran," Millett remembers. Fox Company, still in the ditch at the side of the road, watched the whole spectacle with amazement. They didn't move.

Millett received a Distinguished Service Cross for his actions that day. But it would be another two days before Easy Company's most historic contact with the enemy would occur—a contact that produced the last infantry charge in U.S. military history.

On February 6, the battalion task force continued moving forward, tearing into the enemy. Millett's company had earned a rest because of the previous day's action. So today, they watched the task force's flank.

On February 7, Easy Company returned to the front, spearheading the American advance north. Millett had three tanks supporting his men. Around noon, two of the company's platoons were marching down a road toward Hill 180. The third platoon was trekking on a mountain ridge that ran parallel to the road. A ridge ahead lay perpendicular to and separated by a valley from the platoon on the nearby ridge. On this forward ridge, a camouflaged area of brush was spotted by Private First Class Victor Cozares, one of the company's sharp observers. Millett had considered bypassing the perpendicular ridge entirely; but when he was told what Private Cozares had seen, he changed his mind.

Millett brought the first two platoons, with the tanks, up the road toward the ridge. When the troops got closer to the site, Millett jumped onto one of the tanks and fired a .50-caliber machine gun into a position near the top of the mountain. "Keep it going right here!" he told the machine gunner. "Keep firing until you see us halfway up the hill." Millett knew his artillery was too far away from the spot to do any good.

Millett ordered the ridge platoon that was above and to the side of the other two platoons to stay in position and to provide hill-to-hill fire support. The North Koreans could see they were about to be attacked: they started firing on the Americans.

The two platoons on the road scrambled the rest of the way to the base of the ridge to protect themselves from the hostile fire above them. The North Koreans had honeycombed the entire hill with bunkers and foxholes—a hill described later by

Colonel R. Ernest Dupuy as "a human hornet's nest about to vomit grenades and small arms fire" at the attackers.

The men at the base of the hill were taking fire. Millett realized that the attack would be stopped before it started if he didn't do something quickly. He plunged into the middle of his troops and shouted, "Get ready to move out! Fix bayonets! We're up the hill! Everyone goes with me! Charge!" Plunging up the hill, the men followed their commander.

One soldier—Private First Class John W. ("Red") Lescallet—was struck by the blast of a mortar shell as he began his charge up the hill. He was knocked down, got up, and kept charging. Then a bullet struck his machine gun at the latch cover and ruined it. He threw it down, pulled his pistol out, and kept screaming as he continued his charge.

The hillside became frantic with the sounds of screaming attackers running through defenders' bullets and shells. Hand grenades were flying freely. When Millett arrived at the hill's first ridge line, he could see a machine gun nest 250 yards above him on the left. He called for automatic weapons support and was alerted that a foxhole with eight enemy troops was on his right side, less than ten yards away. Millett swung around and shot his M-1 rifle into the enemy position just as Private Jim Chung—one of Easy's South Korean machine gunners—moved in to finish the job with his Browning Automatic rifle. Millett threw in two hand grenades to make sure.

Securing a radio, Millett ordered the ridge platoon down the rear hill to join the attack on Hill 180. Third Platoon began slipping and sliding down their ice-covered ridge. They were ready to join the fight.

By now, one hundred American soldiers were running and screaming up the hill. Millett's men could hear the air stir with thousands of buzzing bullets all around them. "We got to within twenty or thirty feet of the top," remembers Millett. "We started getting shot at by an antitank gun, which was now an antipersonnel problem at the middle of the ridge." This gun fired shells that could penetrate an inch of steel at three rounds per clip.

It had to be stopped. It was. The men ran right over it with a combination of grenades and automatic weapons fire.

One of the men, a Sergeant Hines, yelled to Millett, "Watch out!" There were three enemy soldiers close to him in a foxhole. They were starting to throw out grenades that were connected together. These clusters came down all around, locking five to six grenades at a time. The attackers dodged them the best they could. One skidded along the ground and hit Millett's leg, blowing a piece of his shinbone out.

"I figured that every time they threw grenades, someone had to stand up. And that would be the best time to jump in the hole with them." Millett was the farthest up the hill, so he waited for the next throw. "When I saw an enemy soldier again, I jumped into his hole and jammed my blade into his chest." Millett then stabbed another in the throat just as a third North Korean turned toward him with a submachine gun.

Perhaps hearing Millett's war screams—or maybe just seeing a crazed man with an elegant, flowing, red mustache—caused the enemy soldier to freeze just long enough for Millett to stab him right through the forehead. "I thought a head was harder than that," remembers Millett. "There was no resistance in the bone. It was like stabbing a cantaloupe." Millett then fired a shot to release his steel from the flesh.

As Millett was finishing off the third man, his men entered into a final, headlong, cold-steel charge at the Chinese who were dug in at the top of the hill. The blood-curdling screams of the attackers, and the intensity of the return fire, were unforgetable. The enemy stood up in their foxholes to meet the Americans. Intense hand-to-hand combat ensued. Millett sprung out of the hole and waved his rifle aloft, screaming "She-lie sa-ni! She-lie sa-ni!"—which means, "I'll kill you with my bayonet!" The attacking platoons ripped into the enemy.

Sergeant John Cockrell jumped into a trench and jammed a bayonet down an enemy soldier's neck into his chest. Hot blood spurted into Cockrell's face just as a second enemy soldier jumped forward. The sergeant's bayonet bullet—fired from one foot—hit and stopped the enemy directly between the eyes.

Private Cozares jumped into a ditch just as an enemy soldier met him. Falling forward, he speared his bayonet toward the enemy. His knees hit the dirt as the blade entered his adversary's chest. The sensation and sound was overpowering. The penetration gave a booming percussion "like a big bass drum." Another North Korean tried to crawl away, but Cozares shot him as well, not even bothering to shoulder his rifle.

The screaming and killing continued. Millett described what followed as "insanity." Cozares thrust his bayonet four more times into the dead soldier—each time followed by the same booming percussion. Another unnecessary thrust was made to the enemy's head, which wedged the blade into the skull. Just then, Cozares heard Private First Class "Buddha-head" Shoda pass him through all the confusion, marching slowly up the the hill. He was carrying his Browning Automatic rifle and was methodically firing at every shrub or bit of ground that looked like it might conceal an enemy soldier. Moving slowly in a straight line through the mayhem, and ignoring everything around him, Shoda was laughing—a steady, terrible, continuous laugh. This was insanity.

The men were still screaming uncontrollably. As the search began for any remaining enemy soldiers, Millett told his sergeant, "There will be no prisoners."

Private First Class Cozares found a bunker that was returning intense fire. He stood on the lip of a small ridge and started tossing grenades at the enemy. When he ran out of grenades, the troops below him started passing more up to him. He tossed them, too, until his steady stream of destruction stopped the enemy fire.

The vastly outnumbered Americans pressed forward. For its part, the enemy's strength was vastly reduced. The numbers were being equalized. Panic swept through the remaining enemy soldiers. They tried to get away.

Corporal Bob Faulkner was running past a hole when an
enemy soldier jumped up, rifle in hand. Faulkner charged and
speared his bayonet into the man's neck. The enemy went down
with blood spurting from his wound. But he wasn't dead. For
ten minutes the man lay on the ground, holding his neck in a
losing battle with death. He tried to talk. He tried to gesture,
but no one would help him, or kill him. He just lay there until
he was dead.

The Americans had now taken the hill. They began dancing
a jig with their blood-spattered rifles over their heads. They
chanted, "We're good, we're good, we're good." Shoda's soft
hysterical laughter could still be heard. The bloodletting was
over, but the frenzy was not. "It was like the Vikings when they
plundered villages," remembers Millett. "Seeing a human being
with his head off is a horrible sight. Something terrible has to
happen in a human being to allow him to be a part of something
like this."

The combat lasted less than an hour, and many enemy soldiers were killed. Almost half of them were bayoneted. When
the action ended, Millett called for the tanks to move forward
as artillery support to hold the position. While he was directing
the tanks, Sergeant Don Brockmeier stuck a bayonet into a crev-
ice on the hill with a note that read, "Compliments of Easy
Company." All nine Americans who died that day came from
Sergeant Brockmeier's platoon. In fact, by the time the sergeant
got to the top of the hill, he had no ammunition left. His desperate fight had ended with the bayonet. He earned the right
to place the message.

Millett remembers, "We were ready for a bayonet battle and
we went berserk, crazy. It was a fighting frenzy. A red haze
came over us, and time stood still. We lost control of our actions." After the battle the men felt weak. Many of them couldn't
even stand. "For a time, you become so powerful, you could
rip doors off," remembers Millett. "You have no fear. Reason
and logic are left behind."

Later, Brigadier General S. L. A. Marshall—an observer of the action—described the charge as the "greatest bayonet attack by U.S. soldiers since Cold Harbor in the Civil War." Interviewing the company on the day after the action, Marshall remarked, "It's funny, I've only run into one other episode such as this where Americans in a fight have gone berserk, and emotional control simply vanished. This incident was Millsap's Patrol in the Normandy action during World War II. In this action, the men got so steamed up after killing the Germans, they went on to slaughter the cattle and chickens around the farmhouse." In response, one of Millett's sergeants—although embarrassed—replied, "Colonel, we weren't going to tell you. But that's what happened to us too, you know. The enemy had a bunch of Mongolian ponies staked out on that hill. We slaughtered every last one of them before we were done."

Millett received the Congressional Medal of Honor for his actions on that wintry Korean day. But before that, he received orders never again to attempt such an attack. For the enemies of the United States, it seems, the last American infantry charge had been led.

Millett went on to see more combat in Korea, and later—for six years—in Vietnam. In 1960, he started the U.S. Army Rangers. In 1968, he trained the Meung Tribesmen under General Vang Pao, and formed the Laos Commandos, as well. The Recondos of the 101st and the Raiders of the 82nd Airborne also got their start under Millett's direction.

During his military career, Millett received four Purple Hearts, three Bronze Stars, one Silver Star, one Distinguished Service Cross, and the Medal of Honor.

In a poem about his family, Millett once wrote, "We're proud of the name Millett, / although we are common and ordinary folk. / But we've shed our blood on four continents, / to shun tyranny's yoke." A price must be paid for liberty. It's never bought for nothing. This price has been paid by Freedom's Warrior, Lewis Millett, and by generations of his family.

Part III

ISLANDS

10.

MITCHELL PAIGE

A Hero's Hero

The success of the United States has often been built on the sweat and labor of people from other countries who immigrated here to improve their lives and the lives of their families. Often these people and their children have been at the front of the line when it comes to patriotism and willingness to sacrifice for the country's common good. Mitchell Paige stands among them.

The product of parents from Serbia, Mitch grew up learning about and learning to love the freedom and history of the United States. When the time came for him to give service for his country, he not only did his job; he became a part of its history.

Mitchell Paige
Platoon Sergeant, U.S. Marine Corps
Guadalcanal, the Solomon Islands
26 October 1942

Mitchell Paige made his mark as a Marine. Standing six feet tall, he is a handsome and gentle man who was born on August 31, 1918, in Charleroi, Pennsylvania—twenty-five years and an ocean away from a ridge on a little-known South Pacific island that would distinguish his life forever. His actions there changed a war and determined the course of history.

The son of a railroad construction worker of very modest means, Mitch Paige left home in 1936 to join the Marines. When World War II began, he became a machine gunner in the 7th Regiment of the 1st Marine Division, which landed at Guadalcanal on September 18, 1942.

"We hit the beach with our Higgins boats," Paige recalls. "Going over the sides, we waded onto the beach and quickly moved inland. Immediately we were in battle under steady enemy shelling and bombing. Small arms and sniper fire was a persistent danger."

By the time Mitch's platoon had established itself inland, the Marines had already formed a small perimeter on the island— the result of America's first ground offensive of World War II in the Pacific. The perimeter started at the water's edge and extended over ridges and through the jungle before returning to the ocean. This small area of land was the most important in the South Pacific because within its perimeter was the "gem of the Pacific": Henderson Air Field.

Control of this airfield meant air superiority in the South Pacific. If the Japanese took this prize, the risk of losing Australia and New Zealand would be very real. The airfield had to be held: much depended on these Marines.

On October 24, 1942, Paige's platoon was ordered to take a defensive position on a ridge that had previously been undefended. Unknown to the Marines, the Japanese could see from an observation point on top of Mount Austin that this same bare ridge offered them an opportunity to isolate Henderson Air Field and to divide in half the Matanikau River and the Marine defensive perimeter. This was a key piece of land in the Japanese plan to retake Henderson Field.

Paige and his platoon were proud Marines. Their water-cooled machine guns were second to none. "These were the weapons that Captain Michael Mahoney, Sergeant Bill Agee, and I improved with a special bolt which resulted in an extremely high rate of fire and uncanny accuracy," Paige remembers. "We were the only Marines who had these guns and I would match them with anyone's, anywhere."

Paige moved his machine gun platoon of thirty-three men and four machine guns into position. It was pitch dark. The men had to crawl on their hands and knees to feel the terrain and place the machine guns properly. As usual, it was raining. Enemy incoming artillery and mortar fire passed overhead.

Paige remembers, "In the morning, I looked around, wondering who in the world would ever choose to defend a spot like this." Their position was actually in front of everyone else, which made Mitch's Marines feel like they were out on a diving board. The enemy could hit them from three sides on this ridge. Mitch and his men would still be out front, alone.

Behind Paige's platoon, the ridge sloped down to the ocean. Between the ridge and Henderson Field was the forward command post with the executive officer, Major Odell Conoley. There were only fifteen men available to defend the post, and Mitch's machine gunners knew they had to hold their ground.

A little later in the morning, Major Conoley came up to the ridge and told Paige that his position—this very ridge—was probably where the Japanese would try to breach the Marine lines. "They wouldn't expect us to defend a place like this," he said.

"We strung some barbed wire and placed trip wires connected to ration cans containing spent cartridges to produce noise," remembers Paige. "This was our early warning device. There was nothing else we could do."

That night, Paige was lying on his back and allowing the rain to hit him in the face when he heard noise below and in front of the platoon's position. The empty ration cans were making a racket. Looking down the ridge, he could see little lights from the jungle below. He knew these were enemy squad leaders moving their men into position—readying them for attack.

Paige went from man to man and whispered, "They're coming. Don't fire until they're right on top of us." In setting up his platoon's interlocking fire, Paige had figured that, when the enemy reached a certain point, nothing could get through. But if the Marines fired too early, the attackers would simply pull back and call for mortar fire to blow the Marines from the ridge.

This night—October 25th, 1942—would belong to history.

"Just as sure as anything, the Japanese came out of the jungle," Paige remembers. "They began climbing the hill toward my men who were armed with machine guns and knee mortars. It was pitch black by now. We waited until they got to within a few feet of us. In fact, we could actually smell them."

The machine gunners didn't fire until the Japanese were right on top of them. "There were hundreds of them," Paige recalls. "When they slammed into my men, it seemed like fifty million people were screaming. It was like a tornado had hit."

Paige gave the command to fire, and the Marine line erupted into flame. Artillery and mortar fire screamed overhead. In the darkness, the machine guns began to do their work. Yet some attackers made it through. Grenades were exploding everywhere. Shadows began engaging one another in hand-to-hand combat.

As the Japanese eruption began, things got worse for Paige and his men. Believing they would be annihilated by the enemy charge, the men of Fox Rifle Company withdrew from the left side of Paige's ridge. Their withdrawal left the left flank wide open. Paige saw the men disappear over the crest of the hill behind him.

Picking up a Springfield rifle, he shouted to them to return to their positions and hold the line. Paige even fired a shot in their direction. But they continued to reposition over on the back of the ridge.

The fighting began, changing minute by minute. "There were times when I would lock in combat with a cursing enemy soldier," Paige remembers. "My weapons changed from my knife to a Springfield rifle, and then to someone else's machine gun." The fighting went back and forth for almost five and a half hours throughout the night.

At one point in the darkness, Paige noticed enemy soldiers moving toward the ridge line behind him. The Japanese were now behind what was left of the platoon, and Paige realized that his Marine position had been overrun. "I swung a machine gun around and hit them with a burst. Not one of them . . . not one, made it past the ridge," Paige recalls.

Because Marines in other companies could now see and hear a machine gun firing backward toward the ocean, it was reported to Major General A. A. Vandegrift that Platoon Sergeant Paige and his men had been overrun and enemy soldiers were firing his machine guns.

The battle continued.

Paige recalls the horror of that night: "I ran from machine gun to machine gun, firing each time until I was out of ammo. As the early morning light began, I could see the entire hill covered with bodies." Then, Paige spotted one of the water-cooled machine guns with its gunner dead at its side. He realized he had to reach that gun before the Japanese noticed it.

Paige yelled for the help of some men from Easy Company who were making their way to support the Marines on the ridge. They fixed their bayonets and started running toward Paige. But they fell to the ground when the Japanese saw them and directed their fire at them. Paige kept running. By now, he was jumping over fallen soldiers who were twitching, moaning, and bleeding on this horror-filled battleground. It became a race between him and any enemy soldier who might have seen the unmanned machine gun, which was positioned to control the ridge.

Reaching the gun, Paige slid behind it. Looking straight over the water jacket to the sloping area to his immediate front, he saw an enemy soldier come up and place his Nambu machine gun into position only a short distance to the left of him.

Struggling to load the gun, Paige lifted the cover and dropped the belt of ammo into position. He slid the belt through as quickly as he could and closed the cover. In order to load a water-cooled machine gun, it is necessary to pull the bolt back twice. Leaning forward, Paige pulled the bolt handle to the rear a first time just as the Japanese gunner zeroed in and squeezed his trigger. Paige could hear the chatter of the Nambu, and he actually felt the warmth of a stream of bullets as they went between his chin and Adam's apple. "It was a sensation I'll never forget," Paige remembers.

Paige tried to lean forward to pull his bolt handle to the rear a second time. But he couldn't move forward. It was as if he were being held back by an invisible wall. "I struggled to lean forward, to grab the bolt handle to load my weapon," Paige remembers. "But I couldn't overcome the strange force that was holding me back." Just as the enemy Nambu ran out of ammunition, the strange force released Paige. His upper body fell forward into the path where the bullets had been. Instinctively, Paige grabbed his bolt handle and pulled it back for the second time. Then he swung his gun around and hit the enemy soldier with a full burst of fire, killing him instantly.

At that time, Paige noticed activity at the front of the hill. Swinging the gun back, he raked the area with machine gun fire. Looking around again, he saw that his machine gunners were either dead or wounded—all of them. It was then he decided to go down that hill in front of him—to finish the job.

Paige remembers, "I placed two belts of ammunition over my shoulder, unclamped my water-cooled machine gun from its tripod and cradled it in my arms for attack." Then, calling out to any rifleman for help, Paige charged down the hill into the Kunai grass toward the Japanese.

Some remaining enemy soldiers appeared, surrounding an older Japanese officer who was probably the attackers' battalion commander. Running down the hill into these soldiers, Paige fired a long burst with devastating effect.

The officer came toward Paige, firing his pistol until it was empty. He threw the pistol down in frustration and began to draw his samurai sword. As the force of the officer's attack brought him to within a few feet, Paige again squeezed the trigger of his machine gun, hitting both the officer and the sword with a full burst of fire.

Glancing around, Paige could see no more enemy soldiers. He walked back up the hill and looked at the body of the enemy machine gunner who had come so close to killing him. He sat down in the middle of almost a thousand dead enemy soldiers while steam was still escaping from his water-cooled machine gun.

"Why him and not me?" Paige wondered. "I just sat there."

Mitchell Paige and a single Marine platoon of only thirty-three men had turned back the vicious attack on Henderson Field. By the end of the battle, every one of these men was either dead or wounded. This stand—led by one man against overwhelming enemy forces—was one of the most significant acts of heroism during World War II. It occurred during a time when American land victories were rare.

There exist rare examples in military history when a single man, in a single battle, can affect the course of an entire war. Mitchell Paige, leading his brave platoon, was one such hero.

In early 1943, Paige was presented the Medal of Honor by General Vandegrift at a small ceremony in Australia. There was still a job to be done in the Pacific, and Paige hadn't wanted to go back to the United States and be touted as a hero selling war bonds. Other men could do that. Instead, he decided to go back to his men. He rejoined the fight in New Guinea and the New Britain Islands.

In the fall of 1944, however, President Franklin D. Roosevelt made it official, presenting this country's highest military award—the Congressional Medal of Honor—to Mitchell Paige, a hero's hero.

11.

DIRK J. VLUG

The TD Kid

The horror of combat can do many things to men. Some hide for cover in their foxholes. Others follow their leaders, but never take initiative. Still other men are changed by combat: they step forward and become different people. These men race into the enemy and win battles—battles that eventually win wars.

Dirk Vlug is one of these men. Because he is a quiet person, few people who meet him would consider him a hero, or even a leader. But in combat, he proved to be a man who could lead other men and show the way. Dirk Vlug is one man who became a warrior.

Dirk J. Vlug
Private First Class, U.S. Army
Ormoc Road, Leyte Island, the Philippines
15 December 1944

Dirk Vlug was a member of the 32nd Infantry Division—the most battle-experienced division in U.S. military history. He was drafted in 1941, and went to Camp Livingston, Louisiana, expecting only to do his duty. But he was a soldier who returned home a hero, bringing honor to his unit and pride to the people of Grand Rapids, Michigan.

General George Marshall called the battle for the Philippine island of Leyte "one of the most decisive battles in history." The Japanese had 260,000 men entrenched on these islands, under the command of General Tomoyuki Yamashita. These battle-hardened Japanese troops were charged with the critical defense of the Philippines. They were expecting an Allied attack, but they didn't know when or where.

On October 20, 1944, it came. The Allied landing on Leyte was achieved with initial surprise.

Early on, it became clear that the Japanese were going to make every effort to hold this island. Japanese planes, ships, and troops were rapidly transported to the site. The crack-outfit, battle-hardened Japanese Imperial 1st Division was brought in. Kamikaze air strikes commenced, revealing to the Allies just how important the Japanese considered the island's defense. The Leyte operation would become a vital, decisive climax of the War in the South Pacific.

Vlug remembers, "In November 1944, my company landed on Leyte. This was the seventeenth day after the initial landing, and the fighting was still intense throughout the island. We were sent right to the front line." Even though Vlug's company had seen some action on New Guinea, so far they had lost more men to malaria than to bullets. Leyte would be their first major action.

Vlug was part of an antitank unit consisting of bazookas and rockets that had been ordered to hold a portion of the Ormoc Road, one of the main roads on the island. His battalion was on the receiving end of a squeezing action. U.S. Army troops were on the other side of the island, driving the Japanese toward Vlug's company. The GIs had set up a roadblock. They dug in along the side of the road in foxholes, with a big tree cut down in front of them to keep anything from getting past. They waited.

"We started to hear Japanese tanks coming down the long curving road toward our position," Vlug remembers. "I was back from the front of the roadblock; but when the Japanese tanks rolled into view, I knew I would be needed." Vlug and his sergeant moved up front to meet the tanks with their rocket launchers.

"I could see five tanks coming. And when they got closer, they saw us," Vlug remembers. "They started firing at everybody. They went at us with their cannons and machine guns. Dirt was flying. There were screams and confusion. Guys were getting shot everywhere." Vlug and his sergeant ran to the downed tree at the front of the roadblock.

The tanks started laying down a heavy smoke screen to conceal their movements. They kept firing with heavy machine guns and thirty-seven-millimeter cannons. By now, all the Americans had taken cover from the devastating fire—except Dirk Vlug. He grabbed six rockets and, with his launcher, ran out toward the lead tank under intense fire that was now directed at him.

Vlug remembers, "I ran forward, putting the first tank into my bazooka sight. I fired and got a direct hit." He could hear screams from inside the tank. And for the first time, he realized just how powerful were these weapons he carried.

A second tank came around the corner, firing directly on top of Vlug. Again he aimed—this time a little high. He fired and got another hit. Two fully-camouflaged Japanese soldiers were riding on this tank, and he hit one directly. "That guy was kind of blown apart," Vlug recalls. The other enemy soldier—realizing his ride had ended—made a dash to the smoking first tank. He lifted up the hatch to escape inside, but Vlug stopped him with pistol fire from fifteen yards.

Vlug had now moved quite a ways from the front of his unit's position. Enemy tanks were between him and the roadblock. The rest of his company was still pinned down in the foxholes by the intense machine-gun fire from the remaining tanks. Vlug flanked back and weapon-sighted another tank at the roadblock. He fired, and his third tank was hit.

The remaining two tanks were getting nervous. Three tanks were smoking. The live ones decided to leave—fast. Vlug remembers, "Those two tanks started out of there. One went down an embankment that seemed pretty steep. He got stuck at a tree or something. They say I shot him too, but I don't really remember. There was a lot going on, but I do remember a hole in his smoking turret as I ran by."

Vlug began chasing the only remaining tank, which was trying to break through thick brush to escape him. He recalls, "I didn't think tanks could go through stuff that heavy. But I suppose he had pretty good motivation to get out of there. I followed his tracks for a while and really wanted to get him, but I thought I heard engines above me on the road again."

Vlug called out for more ammunition as he climbed back to the road. His ammunition man came halfway out of a foxhole and threw some more shells in his direction. Vlug reloaded and went down the road where he thought he had heard the engines. There were no more enemy tanks.

Returning to his company, he found the four tanks smoking. The men came out of their foxholes. Vlug now had a new nickname: the "TD Kid." The "TD" stood for Tank Destroyer. Vlug remembers, "I kind of liked the name, and I guess it stuck."

The next night on the road, the men were still hidden in their foxholes. They heard Japanese soldiers come up and check the destroyed tanks. "We had the discipline not to fire," Vlug recalls. "Then another group came by and started fumbling around with the burned-out tanks. Again, they didn't know we were there, and we let them go. We had no desire to start throwing grenades in the dark. It really would have served no purpose."

Within one week, the battle of Leyte Island had ended. The Japanese's last stand concluded with only five hundred men at the command headquarters. A letter written by a Japanese soldier was found at the enemy headquarters after the final battle. It read, "I am exhausted. We have no food. The enemy are now within five hundred meters of us. Mother, my dear wife, and son, I am writing this letter to you by dim candlelight. Our end is near. Hundreds of pale soldiers of Japan are waiting our glorious end and nothing else."

In the two months of battle for Leyte Island, 56,263 Japanese soldiers died. The battle for the Philippines would be lost for the Japanese. The end of the War in the Pacific was near.

"When you're in combat, you really don't think about dying. You're in a battle mode and you have a job to do," says Vlug. "I guess part of what gets into you is the hate you develop for the enemy. They want to kill your friends and they want to kill you. This brings a certain kind of aggressiveness out in a person. But then, there are other times when you are sitting in a foxhole watching an ant crawl by and you start thinking that he has as much right to live as you or your enemy does.

"I'm proud of my citation because it doesn't talk about the seventeen people I killed. It talks about tanks. I guess that makes it less personal. It was war, and people get killed in war. But nobody likes to think about the people they have killed during the hell of war."

On June 14, 1946, President Harry S Truman presented the Congressional Medal of Honor to Dirk Vlug, who had experienced this hell for the sake of his country.

12.

LOUIS HUGH WILSON, JR.

A Career in Taking Hills

The Medal of Honor is given to men who demonstrate uncommon bravery and courage. Sometimes it is given to men who also show exceptional leadership and intelligence. Louis Wilson is one such man.

A competent leader of men during World War II's South Pacific islands attacks, this Marine also showed his abilities during the following thirty years. Advancing through the Marine Corps ranks to become a four-star general, the commandant of the Marine Corps, and a member of President Jimmy Carter's Joint Chiefs of Staff, Louis Wilson has personified leadership for almost five decades.

Throughout the long and distinguished history of the Marine Corps, only thirty men have risen to the rank of commandant. This distinction, combined with the Congressional Medal of Honor, places Louis H. Wilson in a category of men whose military careers are without equal.

He was born February 11, 1920, in Brandon, Mississippi—a town with a population of five hundred. Raised by his mother because his father died when Louis was only five, he was active in sports as a boy. He graduated from Millsaps College in Jackson, Mississippi, and went to Marine Officers Candidate Class. The talk of war was getting pretty loud. By the time he became a Marine second lieutenant, the attack on Pearl Harbor was less than a month away.

When the war started, Wilson was in Quantico, Virginia. He remembers the feeling of excitement and anticipation: "There were three hundred of us, and we were all anxious to take our places as platoon leaders. There was no fear. The country was as one in its patriotism and commitment to defeat the enemy."

Wilson joined the 9th Marine Regiment at Camp Elliot, California, where he became a platoon leader in Fox Company of the 2nd Battalion. These men were sent to New Zealand in early 1943, where they spent six months preparing for battle. Then, in the late summer of 1943, it was on to Guadalcanal. By then, Guadalcanal's landing had already been completed and the island's operations were mostly defensive.

In November 1943, Wilson participated in his first combat beach landing when his company landed with the first wave at Bougainville. "I wasn't afraid of hitting the beaches," says Wilson. "We were well trained, and you could say we anticipated rather than feared the landing. We were young and I think we all had the feeling of invincibility. We thought we couldn't die, even though we saw a lot of our friends die."

By now, Wilson was getting a reputation as a "gung ho" officer. He knew he was good at what he did, and he felt he had a future in the Marine Corps. "I knew I was a capable officer," says Wilson. "I was one of a group of junior officers in the division who did their jobs a little better than the others." Wilson was also earning the respect of fellow soldiers—not only from his superiors and other lieutenants, but also from the soldiers he led.

After Bougainville, Wilson and his company went back to Guadalcanal to rest and rearm. Wilson was promoted to captain. His company would soon be involved in the landing on Guam.

The landing occurred on July 21, 1944. "We transferred onto an LVT just off the reef and drove the rest of the way to the beach in this amphibious vehicle," remembers Wilson. "A lot of men were dying on those beaches. Bougainville didn't have reefs to worry about, so this kind of landing was new to us."

Wilson's company came in on the right side of the landing force. Their initial objective was to take a Navy yard that the Marines had used before the war. Overlooking this beach landing was the strategically important Fonte Hill. This two-thousand-foot hill was the tallest on the island. The Marines didn't know the Japanese were using Fonte Hill as their headquarters for the entire island's defense. The Marines did know the hill had to be taken.

"It ended up taking us three days to even get there," Wilson remembers. On July 25, Wilson received his orders from the battalion commander to take Fonte Hill. The hill was surrounded by heavy jungle, so it wasn't clear where the enemy might be hidden. It was also raining.

"In the late afternoon, we attacked," remembers Wilson. "Waves of Japanese began coming over the hill right into us." The company commanders on both sides of Wilson were killed as the attack began, and the remnants of those two companies came under his command. Wilson became the commanding officer of the Fonte Hill attack.

"By dark, we could no longer see the enemy. I called for flares from our ships," Wilson recalls. "They gave us some. But it turned out they were being fired short: the flares ended up silhouetting us, but not the Japanese." Wilson tried to establish communication with the ships to get the flares in farther. He couldn't.

Early in the attack Wilson was shot in his right knee and shoulder. Machine gun bullets had gone completely through both the front and the back of his knee. But he could still walk and he refused medical treatment. Wilson bandaged over his wounds and continued leading the hill attack.

Early into the night—five hours after the Marine attack had begun—the hill was finally taken at great cost. Wilson immediately began organizing a defensive perimeter at the top, ordering his men to dig foxholes. He knew the Japanese weren't done with them yet.

And sure enough, the Japanese renewed their torrent of fire into the Marines. Then the vicious counterattacks began. Wilson could see a slight elevation—just to the right of their hilltop—that was still held by Japanese snipers who were maintaining a constant fire into the Marine position. Wilson remembers, "We could hear the Japanese yelling at us throughout the night. And at times, we would see enemy soldiers waving their saki bottles before they threw them down and charged."

During the night battle, one of Wilson's gunnery sergeants—a man with twenty-five years' service—was hit in front of the Marine defensive perimeter. He was about fifty yards in front, yelling that he was hit. By this time, it seemed as if everyone was calling out that they were hit. The medics had their hands full.

Wilson began crawling through the fire. He made it to the wounded Marine, and started to drag him back. "He was just a little guy, weighing no more than a hundred pounds soaking wet," remembers Wilson. "I can't really say we were being fired on the whole way, but we were being fired on. We weren't hit, though, and we made it back."

Wilson still had about 150 men from the original three companies on the top of the hill. "We had taken rather extensive casualties," remembers Wilson. "We had no artillery support, and there were no reinforcements to call in. We were on our own."

Wilson didn't think they were going to make it until morning. He remembers the fear he felt as the Japanese continued attack after attack throughout the night. It wasn't always clear who was in charge of the hill.

"That night, anything that moved was considered Japanese," Wilson says. "Anything that moved got shot. One time, I looked up and saw someone bending over, looking into my foxhole. I immediately shot him with my .45. It was a Japanese lieutenant, and I took his sword."

There were no clearly identified front lines. The Japanese didn't have any clearer picture of what was going on than Wilson did. "Combat is not like you see in the movies," says Wilson. "It's confusion. You're lying in your foxhole, hoping to live, and you shoot your gun at whatever moves. The fact is, I was a strong captain in charge of the hill, and most of the time throughout that night of battle, I didn't know what was going on. Nobody did."

The Marines survived the Japanese counterattacks. The next morning, Wilson and his men were saved by a group of tanks that moved to the front of the hill and began firing on the surrounding enemy. "We actually watched one drunken Japanese jump on top of a tank," Wilson remembers. "I think he was a Japanese officer because he had a sword, which he began using to slash at the tank turret. I remember my Marines arguing, 'Stop. Let me shoot him,' 'No, let me.' Finally, one of them did."

Things were still far from secure on the hill. With the morning's tank advance, the Japanese had pulled back their main attacks. But they still surrounded the Marines, and the exchange of gunfire had not stopped. Wilson's big problem now was another elevation about sixty-five feet above and to the right of them. The Japanese still held this elevation, and they continued shooting down into the Marines with devastating effect. Now that it was light, Wilson knew, this ridge had to be cleared of Japanese snipers.

Wilson took seventeen men and started toward the enemy stronghold. Says Wilson, "I'd like to tell you I chose those men, or that they were part of my reserve force. But the truth is, they were all the men I could find in my area. So I took them, and we charged."

Through intense mortar, machine gun, and rifle fire, Wilson led those seventeen brave Marines toward the ridge that had been plaguing and killing his men all night. Thirteen of his men were shot during the charge, but nonetheless the enemy soldiers were overrun. Only four Marines stood at the top of the ridge by the time the fight ended.

By now, though, the Marines had reinforcements fighting their way up the front of the hill. The beleaguered Japanese attackers began pulling out. Wilson and his tired men were relieved by a battalion of reinforcements. The high-priced gains of the previous twenty-four hours were secured.

Wilson and his Marines went down the front of the hill and had a hot meal. Then, in the warmth of a Guam summer night, they lay down to sleep.

More than 350 Japanese soldiers were dead on Fonte Hill. The most strategic position in Guam, as well as the island's Japanese headquarters, had been taken and held by this small group of fierce Marines led by Captain Wilson.

"Basically, I had good men with me on that hill, and those men did their jobs," says Wilson. "Afterwards, I knew something significant had happened. I ended up getting the credit for this action when Truman presented me with the Medal of Honor, but this was an award deserved by those men for their actions that night and day."

After the Guam action, Wilson spent nearly two months in the hospital, first in Hawaii and then in San Diego. He had been wounded three times in the battle. During a leave, he married his beautiful girlfriend, the former Jane Clark. Peace had broken out, but Captain Wilson's career was just beginning.

"My peacetime career was routine," understates Wilson. "I was ambitious and I did those things that were necessary for my advancement in the military, but I was never consumed by this. I was always in the top 10 percent of the officer ranks, and I knew I would eventually become a general. I guess you could say I did my share of 'ticket punching.' "

Wilson went to the best military schools—for instance, the National War College. He served as aide-de-camp for the three-star general who commanded the Pacific Fleet Marine Force. And later, he became the commanding officer of the Basic School at Quantico—one of the best jobs for a colonel in the Marines. His competence was apparent in whatever he did, and his dedication was clear.

"Throughout my career I have always been 100-percent Marine," says Wilson. "I am a disciplinarian and I was serious about my jobs. I always had my friends, too. I liked to hunt and play golf, which I often did with other officers."

In 1975, Louis Wilson received his fourth star and was appointed by President Gerald Ford to become the commandant of the Marine Corps. He remained on the Joint Chiefs of Staff until he retired four years later.

"When I became commandant of the Marine Corps, we were going through an interesting time," remembers Wilson. "I dealt with a lot of disciplinary problems, and I decided to get rid of the Marines who didn't need to be there." Wilson felt that Marines had to meet certain high standards—standards of fitness and discipline. He gave men two chances and then they were out. If they were out of shape or if they didn't meet Wilson's expectations of Marine behavior, they left.

But Wilson's discipline had to make sense. "Once we had difficulties at the Marine Recruiting Depot," Wilson remembers. "In the name of discipline, one of the recruits was actually beaten to the extent that he died. A drill instructor actually watched this!"

Until this incident, Wilson hadn't realized the extent to which drill instructors were abusing recruits. "I was not prepared to face my recruits' mothers and tell them we would treat their sons worse than we would treat an animal or an enemy," says Wilson.

The harshness of Marine training had gotten out of hand, and General Wilson decided to see it controlled. "You hear the old Marines talking about how hard they had it during basic training. But most of the stories they tell are stories they heard from others and just keep passing on. There is no reason or need to be abusive to men who want to become Marines. Discipline without reason doesn't make men tougher or better."

Wilson made sure the Marine drill instructors understood how he felt. If they insisted on hitting a recruit, Wilson made sure they understood they had reached their terminal rank. "I wouldn't even tolerate them yelling face-to-face with a recruit," says Wilson. "Abuse doesn't teach anything useful. But if anyone thinks the Marines went soft on their recruits, let me ask them if they would be willing to go through basic training at Parris Island. I sure wouldn't. There is still nothing easy about becoming a Marine." The proud traditions survive.

Since retiring as a four-star general in 1979, Wilson has remained active. He served on the Merrill Lynch board of directors for eleven years and still serves on the boards of the Fluor Corporation and of Louisiana Land and Exploration. He lives with his wife of forty-seven years, Jane, near Pasadena, California.

"I've had such a good life—not only in the military, but also with my health and family," says Wilson. "I still can't believe I have been so fortunate." Good fortune, a successful lifelong career, and a character described by honor, bravery, and competence. A true American hero—this is Louis H. Wilson.

Part IV

WATER

13.

DONALD KIRBY ROSS

Pearl Harbor Hero

Devotion to an ideal or to one's fellow man cannot be taught. During the 1930s, men trying to escape the horrors of the Depression were fortunate if they were good enough to be in the military. One such man was Donald Ross, an experienced career sailor who was working the USS Nevada's boilers the morning the Japanese struck Pearl Harbor. Displaying a combination of skill, daring, and devotion to his men, Don Ross not only saved many lives, but helped to save a battleship during this fierce and famous battle.

Donald Kirby Ross
Machinist, U.S. Navy
USS *Nevada*,
Pearl Harbor, Territory of Hawaii
7 December 1941

The big ships of the 1st Battleship Division—the *Arizona*, *Oklahoma*, and *Nevada*—had just returned to Pearl Harbor after conducting night battle practice in the open sea. The date was December 5, 1941.

A young machinist warrant officer on the *Nevada*, Don Ross, had entered the naval service in 1929 and risen through the ranks. He was the watch officer of the engineering department and was responsible for the proper running of the ship's engines and generators. He was capable of taking the ship to sea, and he took his job seriously.

At midnight on Saturday, December 6, Ross relieved his chief in engineering and was told, "Put the engine room on alert. We need to be ready to answer bells with only a half-hour notice by morning." Ross suspected trouble, but his chief didn't tell him any more. The young machinist certainly didn't know that his actions the next day were going to become a part of history.

Ross followed his chief's orders and started heating up the boilers throughout the night. By 0500 hours, he had a "ready condition," with two boilers on full steam and two more coming on line. He gave the order to start shifting boilers.

Ordinarily, a battleship required at least three and a half hours to be under way from a cold start. That morning by 0730, however, the *Nevada* was ready to go with only thirty minutes' notice.

It was Sunday, December 7, 1941.

Ross remembers the morning of the "day that lives in infamy." "I had breakfast in the warrant officers' mess. Then I started getting ready for church by laying out my summer white uniform and shaving. I was half shaven when I heard airplanes screaming outside my porthole. It was 0755."

Ross put his razor down and looked out. He saw three Japanese Zeros racing over the airstrip of Ford Island. They seemed to be firing hot flame right at people going to church on the island. "Then I heard a hell of a big boom. I didn't know what it was," Ross remembers. "I looked at the south end of the island and more Zeros were shooting at the flying boats moored there. A big plume of smoke was coming from the gasoline storage area."

Ross quickly pulled his head back in and slammed the porthole closed. He called the chief's quarters and reported the attack, although that probably wasn't necessary. Then Ross remembers, "I collected my thoughts and actually finished shaving before I ran down to the engine room."

Even though all of the ship's senior officers were ashore, within three minutes Ensign Joseph Taussig had placed the ship on Condition Zed. This was full-combat general quarters. Bombs began hitting American planes on the ramps, and gas tanks were blowing everywhere. The flying boats were being hit; their fuel storage facility was already burning.

Hell was in session.

Ross took charge of the engine room and immediately received a call from the bridge. Chief Quartermaster Bob Sedberry, a seventeen-year veteran of the *Nevada*, demanded, "How long before we can get under way?" Ross answered, "We'll be ready to answer bells in thirty minutes." "That's not possible!" Sedberry replied. The chief quartermaster didn't realize the engine room had been getting ready all night. Ross said, "I'm telling you, I'll be ready to answer bells in thirty minutes." And he was.

Ross requested relief from Chief Warrant Engineer Jack Garrett, so he could get to the forward generators where he was needed most. At 0805, the *Nevada* was hit by a torpedo.

Ross remembers, "When the torpedo hit, it knocked me off the ladder going down to the forward generator room. My fireman snickered when he saw me fall, and cracked, 'What are you trying to do, boss—break the floor plates?' "

When that torpedo blew, the deck watch shifted back. A hole sixty feet long and eighteen feet below the waterline was opened on the port bow of the ship near turret two, only forty feet from the forward dynamo room. "That shook things up a bit," Ross remembers.

The Nevada started taking on water, developing a five-degree list to the starboard side. Ross ordered a shift of oil and the flooding of port "void" compartments to correct the list.

Deep inside the Nevada, Ross had his headphones on, and he could hear the ship's radio communications. Occasionally a circuit would open to the outside, and he could hear the sound of angry airplanes and their killing bombs.

At 0807, Ross heard a tremendous explosion. The sound and feel of this impact far exceeded anything he had ever heard or felt. He didn't know until later that the Arizona—which was moored directly at the Nevada's bow—had just been blown up, killing more than eleven hundred sailors.

Ross recalls, "We finally got control of the situation. The list was off the ship, and we were almost ready to move." But the forward generator room was heating up. Heavy smoke started filling the compartment where Ross and his men were working.

There was a line communications technician monitoring all the dynamo rooms. He reported to Ross that the rear dynamo room was in better condition. Because of the increasing smoke and heat, Ross decided to transfer power to the rear dynamo room as soon as possible. He just needed a little more time for the rear units to get ready.

There were twenty-seven men with him, deep in the bowels of the Nevada. They were running the generators and air compressors to give the ship power to fire its guns and move out. Ross kept his men focused on their job, and not on their fear.

Outside—in another world—the Japanese were strafing the Nevada. So far, their main concentration was on the battleships on Ford Island's Battleship Row, and on Hickam and Wheeler airfields. The flying boats were knocked out, and confusion was everywhere.

By 0832, the *Nevada* was ready to move.

The fleet CINC-PAC, Admiral William Rea Furlong, ordered, "Fleet Sorté!" This directed the ships out to sea as fast as possible to avoid the concentration of the Japanese attack. The *Nevada* headed for the channel that would take her to the safety of the open sea.

As his ship started passing the burning *Arizona*, Ensign Taussig was standing on the *Nevada*'s bridge. He remembers, "The Japanese could see us start to move, and they began concentrating their attack on us. Everything came our way, but we kept firing back." The heat from the burning *Arizona* was so intense that sailors on the *Nevada*'s starboard side took first- and second-degree burns as they passed. The *Nevada*'s gunners refused to leave their guns even though, by now, there were at least fourteen fires burning on the ship. History will record that every one of the *Nevada*'s ten guns kept firing throughout the attack and every one of the ship's gun captains was eventually killed, as were more than half of her initial gunners. The ship was filled with brave men.

Some cruisers and destroyers made it out of the harbor. But as the *Nevada* approached the channel entry, Admiral Harold Train on the battleship *Maryland* could see the escaping battleship's boiling smoke and noticed that she was running low in the water. Concerned that the ship would sink and block the channel entrance, he ordered the *Nevada* to go no farther than the floating dry docks. She would not escape the Japanese attackers.

A new group of Japanese dive bombers started hitting the *Nevada*. The Japanese air commander, Lieutenant Commander Fuchida, was flying in a command plane over Pearl Harbor. Fuchida remembers, "We started to attack again in the midst of their intense antiaircraft fire. This second wave of attackers consisted of 171 planes, and a good number of them headed straight for the *Nevada*, which we could see was trying to escape." It was 0900.

A group of nine planes attacked. The *Nevada* was immediately hit with three bombs. She started taking forward water. A port list developed, and the ship came to a complete stop.

A fourth bomb flew down on the armor deck at the "bull ring" where the ship's air was centralized from the topside for both human breathing and the boilers. When the bomb hit, the engineering spaces were blasted. Ross was standing under a ventilator and received a full blast of fire into his face. His left eye was blinded, and his right eye started burning from the smoke.

Ross momentarily lost consciousness. Then, recovering, he realized the danger to his men. He shouted the order, "Get out, men! Get the hell out of here! Get out! Get out!" The men rushed up the ladder out of the smoky room. Now nothing could be seen in the forward dynamo room because of the intense smoke. The temperature had increased to 140 degrees.

The forward generators were not ready to transfer to the aft generators. Someone needed to stay and do the work of the entire generator crew that had been ordered to leave. Ross stayed behind.

Alone in the hot smoke-filled forward dynamo room, Ross fought to keep the generators working. He also fought to get air. Pulling his shirt off, Ross dipped it into some water and wrapped it around his face. It was pitch dark, and the smoke and heat were getting more and more intense.

Ross knew his eyes were injured. But because it was so smoky, he didn't know he was blinded. The engine "snipes" regularly practiced in complete dark, and Ross knew his way around. "I could find my way anywhere in that room by feel alone," Ross remembers.

If the *Nevada* had lost power in the forward dynamo room then, the whole ship would have been sitting dead in the water during this fierce battle. The guns would have slowed, the pumps would have stopped, and all communication would have been lost. The battleship's very survival depended on the efforts of this brave young officer.

In the terrible heat and smoke, Ross knew he couldn't last

much longer. He started gagging. The aft generators were finally ready; he switched to them as he started to fall. A radio circuit was flipped open and an electrician on the distribution board heard a faint "God help me," followed by gagging, heaving, and then silence.

The electrician immediately called control and said, "Mr. Fee, I think Ross is dead." Chief Engineer Gus Fee, who had taken over main control, returned, "Get him out." The young electrician stripped his phone off, opened the hatch, and jumped into the 140-degree heat and smoke of the forward generator room.

The young sailor quickly found the unconscious Ross and put the officer over his shoulder. Struggling, the sailor worked his way up the eighteen-foot ladder to safety. At the top, he pushed Ross through the hole and then dragged him to the central station. Ross was not breathing.

Artificial respiration was started and went on for several minutes. Slowly, Ross started breathing again. "I didn't know I was out and I didn't know what they were doing to me," Ross says. When he regained consciousness, a terrible realization occurred to him: the exhaust in the forward condenser had not been secured. This could cause a devastating explosion. Struggling to find his way back down into the darkness of the deadly smoke and heat where he had almost died, Ross found the cutoff valve and turned it. The ship was saved.

Ross felt his way out and went back to the central distribution room. From there, he moved down the ninety-foot passageway to the aft dynamo room where he was needed.

When the admiral had ordered the Nevada to avoid the channel entrance, the ship—with the help of a couple of tugs—had started around the island to Hospital Point, where she nosed in. From there, the Nevada backed herself onto a coral reef at a cane field, so she wouldn't sink. It was now 0940 and the attack was ending.

By the time Ross arrived in the aft dynamo room, there was smoke and not enough steam. Saltwater was getting into the boilers, causing them to lose power. Ross began shifting from one boiler to the other. The smoke and heat started to intensify, and a safety line was placed on Ross. "Again, I couldn't see, but I could feel," he remembers.

Ross began a watch in the aft dynamo room and started switching the watch between his men. Each shift could only last a half hour because of the smoke and heat. This work continued throughout the day and into Sunday night.

During one of the shifts, Ross heard that Chief Machinist's Mate "Tommie" Thompson was overcome with smoke. Ross quickly went down with a safety line and found his unconscious chief. He placed Thompson on his shoulder and started climbing back up the ladder.

When Ross got about eight feet up, he himself succumbed to the smoke, and dropped his chief. Ross fell off the ladder unconscious, but was saved by the safety line, which the men on top quickly pulled up. Again he came to. Two other members of the rescue team immediately dropped to the bottom of the ladder and brought the unconscious chief to safety, where he was immediately resuscitated.

The attack on Pearl Harbor lasted only two hours, but the snipes on the *Nevada* had to continue their battle. The *Nevada* was flooding from the huge forward hole made by the torpedo, and the pumps were struggling to keep the ship alive. Ross remembers that miserable night as his men worked to keep the boilers and generators going. "Everyone was fighting, but we were becoming a flooding job. We couldn't get enough pumps to pump out the forward water, which then started to flow into the dynamo room. We were on the coral reef now, so we wouldn't sink; but we didn't want to lose our generators."

As hard as the men worked, the battle eventually ended when the engine room flooded. But the *Nevada* and her generators held off long enough for the ship to save itself for another day. That day, no other ship fought back harder than the *Nevada*.

Although fifty-seven of the ship's brave sailors died that morning during the torpedo hit and five direct bomb hits, miraculously nobody died in the engine and generator rooms. "We used a lot of gas masks made of wet cloths that day," Ross recalls.

By 0600 the next morning, Ross was ordered to sick bay. "I was exhausted. I lay down and the doctor examined my eyes and said I needed to go to the hospital." By this time, Ross had a complete loss of vision in his left eye and could see only light with his right eye. His vision didn't fully return until six months later.

Looking back at his Pearl Harbor experience, Ross remembers, "I didn't think about fear. I was frightened, but the fear didn't control me. The most important thing was my men and the ship. These were more important to me than my own life."

A person is fortunate if, during the course of life, something becomes more valuable than life itself. The *Nevada*—and the snipes in the *Nevada* engine rooms on December 7, 1941—was that something for Donald Ross. Through his efforts that day, the *Nevada* and her men lived to see more days—days of service to their country in the Aleutian Islands, the North Atlantic, and the beaches of Normandy.

On April 18, 1942, Admiral Chester Nimitz presented to Donald K. Ross the Congressional Medal of Honor, this country's highest award. World War II began, for America, at Pearl Harbor. And the day would never be forgotten, for its history and for its heroes.

14.

MICHAEL EDWIN THORNTON

The SEAL

Often, the action that leads to a Medal of Honor involves the taking of lives. However, bravery is also measured in lives saved. Michael Thornton was an experienced and proficient SEAL. He knew how to take the lives of his enemy when he needed to. But he also knew devotion to his fellow SEALs. And when the time came, he showed this devotion during circumstances that reasonable people would have run away from. Because of his brave actions and incredible physical strength, men lived who would otherwise have died.

Michael Edwin Thornton
Petty Officer, U.S. Navy
Republic of Vietnam
31 October 1972

Mike Thornton worked hard in school, but it didn't seem to matter.

Born March 23, 1949, in Greenville, South Carolina, Mike never went to college. In fact, he barely made it through high school. No one could figure it out. Mike studied harder than other students, but he couldn't do well. Other students would breeze through tests while he struggled. He was far from dumb, and he had a lot of common sense. He just couldn't get good grades.

Mike didn't discover the reason for this until much later: he had dyslexia; his brain couldn't interpret what he read, because it saw things backward. Mike started missing classes. In fact, during his senior year of high school, he missed fifty-six days of school. "I think my teachers let me graduate just to get me out of there," explains Mike.

His dad and hero, Edwin G. Thornton, had grown up in a very poor family during the Depression. He only made it through the sixth grade, because he had to take care of his family. Hard work and responsibility were expected in the Thornton family. And the virtue of patriotism was taught.

Mike Thornton joined the Navy after high school in 1967. "My father taught me that the American flag and the national anthem were important symbols," says Thornton. "We have a country to be proud of, and I wanted to do my part."

Thornton was sent to boot camp in San Diego and then to underwater demolitions training. He became a Navy SEAL. Of the 129 men who started the SEALs' rigorous eighteen-week training program in sea, air, and land operations, only twelve men finished. Assigned to SEAL Team One in 1968, Thornton moved to Coronado, California, where his training continued. Each SEAL platoon had two officers and twelve enlisted men.

Thornton was his team's machine gunner and weapons specialist.

A few months later, Thornton went to Vietnam for his first six-month rotation. His unit's assignment was to run special operations—intelligence gathering and disruption of the Vietcong infrastructure. SEAL patrols consisted of four to seven men and lasted up to two weeks.

Thornton's team found and interrogated province chiefs who were running supply routes for the Vietcong. Sometimes they captured enemy soldiers. Other times they would get information about high-level enemy meetings, and then ambush or capture the Vietcong officials.

Often there would be firefights when the team went into the villages to disrupt meetings. Prisoners would be taken and used to get information about other meetings, people, or supply routes. Sometimes the SEALs would be brutal to get information from their prisoners.

"On my first tour I had fear, but it was fear used to my advantage," remembers Thornton. "Being scared makes you operate efficiently. You take your time and you don't push too hard. My fear was like having a security jacket."

Thornton remembers the first time he killed someone: "We were near Ben Luc, seven clicks [kilometers] up a river. There was a firefight in a village when we tried to capture a Vietcong official. He had eight body guards, and they fought back. They shouldn't have."

Thornton continues, "I never lost sleep about the people I killed. They were the enemy. Sometimes the enemy were women and boys, but they were trying to kill me or my team members. In fact, sometimes the women were the most brutal soldiers of all. I wasn't thinking about age when I shot a twelve-year-old boy who was shooting at me with his AK-47."

Once a SEAL team was formed, they would live together, both in Vietnam and in the States. This developed a sense of camaraderie in the men. In 1968, there were only two hundred men in the Navy SEALs. These men knew they were special.

Mike Thornton was considered one of the most physically strong SEALs. Some of the men who worked with him have described him as the strongest man they ever knew. He was good in the field, he was trusted, and he got the job done. During his first Vietnam tour, Thornton became experienced in combat operations. His leadership skills were apparent to everyone who worked with him.

After returning home, Thornton resumed his training. He went to intelligence school, foreign weapons school, improvised demolitions school, and advanced medicine and field medicine schools.

When he returned to Vietnam in 1969, he went as an advisor. He worked with other SEALs, but also with civilians and South Vietnamese troops. Often, he operated by himself outside small villages, knocking out North Vietnamese supplies and organizing ambushes.

He also started working with mercenaries. Some of these men were pretty good soldiers. On his second Vietnam rotation, Mike Thornton had fewer people to worry about. It was easier for him to get in and out of situations. He was either alone or with very small, quick units.

Once, he led a small team deep into "Indian country" to kidnap a Vietcong province chief. He was working with a captured Vietcong district chief who had been "convinced"—for family reasons—to cooperate. Steve Frisk was the only other American with Thornton, and they were hidden in the bottom of a sampan going down a Vietcong-controlled river. Besides the Vietcong cooperator, the team also had three other Vietnamese on the sampan—one who had a concealed weapon directed at their tour guide. "We went through three different check stations where our Vietcong prisoner had to give a password," remembers Mike. "We had this district chief doing all the talking."

The sampan made its way down the river with no problems, and the Vietcong suspected nothing. The district chief was "cooperating," all right. The sampan was lined with bags of rice for two reasons: to conceal the two American SEALs (who were also under rice mats), and to serve as a barrier, if a firefight should occur. The rice turned out to be a good idea.

Eventually, the sampan was stopped by the province chief who was the target of the operation. The province chief asked what was in the boat. The hostage district chief answered, "This is a business sampan."

Then one of the Vietnamese soldiers signaled Thornton with a slight kick. He stood up with his weapon and demanded that the chief and the body guards flanking him on both sides hold up their hands. One of the guards went for his weapon. He shouldn't have. "I greased all three," Thornton remembers. "Then we were in a world of trouble. Bullets started coming in from all over. We were deep in 'bad man' territory and we had to go all the way back up the river through the Vietcong checkpoints."

The raiders cranked up their sampan and, with the bullets flying, started racing up the river. By now, both of the sampan's M-60 machine guns were firing, and air support had been called. Helicopters came from all over. The sampan, racing through exploding fire from both sides of the river, made it out of there.

Mike Thornton's third tour in Southeast Asia was to Thailand, beginning in November 1970. His missions were mostly covert operations that consisted of enemy "body snatches" and training Thai people to do recon missions. Most operations on this rotation remain classified.

By the time his fourth tour started in July 1972, most Americans had already left Vietnam. Thornton—an E-5 now—was stationed near North Vietnam, and his mission was recon and downed-pilot rescue. Downed-pilot missions weren't usually very successful. In fact, the only pilots ever pulled out of North Vietnam were rescued by SEAL Tommie Norris—a feat for which he later received a Medal of Honor.

Mike Thornton's recon missions into North Vietnam were conducted by three to eight men, with at least two Americans among them. "We would determine the types of ordnance the enemy had, their gun emplacements, their strength, and whether they had tanks and trucks to move personnel."

On one special operations mission, Thornton was patrolling up a river, and the unit ran into an NVA ambush. He remembers, "We were surrounded and in a world of trouble. I laid down a base of fire, but one of our KCS [Kit Carson scouts] got hit as we were withdrawing." Thornton ran toward the advancing enemy and grabbed the wounded soldier. Carrying the soldier over his shoulders and walking backward through the mud, Thornton fired his weapon from the hip. "I kept firing like this for over a click," remembers Thornton. "We finally made it back to our perimeter." The Kit Carson scout was saved, and Mike Thornton had developed a technique that would later save one of his best friends.

"During my time in Vietnam, I turned down two Purple Hearts because I didn't think I had been sufficiently wounded," says Thornton. "To me, a Purple Heart should be given when someone has significant and life-threatening injuries. One of the Purple Hearts I turned down was for a shrapnel wound in my back, and another was for a bullet that grazed my scalp and took a chunk out of my head."

Thornton's Medal of Honor action occurred in North Vietnam. By the fall of 1972, most American ground forces were out of Vietnam, and one of Thornton's friends, Tommie Norris, had gone to Saigon to be briefed on a mission.

"We were supposed to recon an area at the Qua Viet River near the Quang Tri Province," remembers Thornton. "It was Halloween, October 31, 1972, and the NVA had taken this area over." He and Tommie Norris were ordered to see how suitable the river would be for an amphibious attack. A successful operation could mean going back to the peace negotiations and using the land won as a bargaining chip. "We understood the significance of this mission when we left," says Thornton.

This high-priority mission seemed spooked from the beginning. The team consisting of Thornton, Norris, and three South Vietnamese special operations soldiers—named Quan, Dang, and their officer Thai—went north to a small South Vietnamese riverine base called Tua Non. Wearing their usual Levis and sweatshirts, with absolutely no identification, the group boarded two Vietnamese junks about forty feet long, and started up the coast in the late afternoon. "We suspected our skipper didn't know where he was," remembers Thornton. "It turned out he didn't." Eight hours into the trip, the Vietnamese boat skipper couldn't find the point where the Qua Viet River empties into the ocean.

Thornton used a night-vision scope on the landscape, to no avail. A ship at sea was supposed to be vectoring their position. But for some reason, this didn't happen, either. The SEALs couldn't get a good reading to find out where they were.

"Don't worry, I know how to get there," the South Vietnamese junk skipper kept saying. "Don't worry." The unit was finally put out in their rubber boats. The skipper said they were about five clicks south of the river. "We paddled in," remembers Thornton. "When we got to the surf zone, we jumped off and started into the beach. I saw no one, and the beach looked safe. We ran to a bush line."

By now, it was the middle of the night. The team found a safe place in the bushes. Thornton and Norris pulled out their map and tried to figure out where they were. There was a dim moonlight that night. Norris pointed and said, "If we are where we're supposed to be, we'd see the Qua Viet River there." Not only was the river not there; it turned out they were actually ten clicks north of the river, rather than just south of it. But they didn't know that yet.

Norris wanted to go into the hills and try to find the river there. The team went inland and started their recon. About eight clicks in, they started to see signs of a large enemy force. They saw enemy gun emplacements and large NVA bunkers. "We were walking right through these guys," remembers Thornton. "We saw their guns and their communications wires, but the real hint came when we saw the NVA soldiers sleeping all around us." Because of the large size of the enemy bunkers,

Thornton and Norris knew they were farther north than they should have been. Bunkers this size could never have survived closer to the border.

"We were walking right through their camp," says Thornton. "We tried to keep as close to the tree line as we could, but we probably were seen by some of the soldiers. Nothing happened, though, because it was too incredible for any enemy soldiers to believe we would walk through their camp. Our boldness was probably our best protection."

The team did a loop through the North Vietnamese camp and started back to the beach. There was at least a battalion strength of NVA troops there. This would be important information back in Saigon.

Because daylight was only a few hours away, the team needed to find a place to hide. They were walking down to a riverbed and—looking up at a hill right next to them—Thornton whispered to Norris, "Tommie, look up there and don't tell me that's a tank sitting there with a big red star on it." Norris looked up the hill and then looked back at Thornton and whispered, "Mike, that's a tank up there and it has a big red star on it." "That's what I didn't want to know," remembers Thornton.

The team got under a tree line and started into the riverbed leading back out to the ocean. The men thought they could find a good place to hide along the shore. They found a big dune area separating the ocean from a huge swamp. Farther inland from the swamp was a line of trees. The men found a small area in the dunes where they could hide, and they lay down.

"We thought we were far enough away from the NVA camp," remembers Thornton. "We were well hidden and just starting to relax when we saw two guards coming down the beach toward us." One guard was at the water's edge, walking ahead of the other, who was three hundred yards inland and walking directly toward the team's hiding place in the dunes. They may have been patrolling or they may have been simply looking for rice supplies that were sometimes dropped off on the beach by supply boats.

Thornton whispered that he'd grab the guard walking toward them if they were seen, and he told the South Vietnamese officer, Thai, to shoot the other guard immediately if this happened. Otherwise, everyone was supposed to be very quiet.

"We waited and, to my relief, the guards started walking by us," recalls Thornton. "Just as I was becoming comfortable that we were not going to be seen, Thai stood up and yelled for the guard by the water to drop his gun. He was actually trying to arrest him."

The guard by the ocean—a little shocked at first—lifted his rifle and started firing. Thornton stood up and slammed his rifle butt into the head of the closer guard and then returned fire. Seeing he was outnumbered, the guard by the ocean started running toward the woods, with Mike Thornton chasing him. "We were in trouble now, because everyone could hear the firing—and they were on their way," Thornton recalls.

Thornton chased the guard until he got to the tree line. At least fifty more NVA soldiers had arrived and began firing. Thornton turned around and started running back to the dunes. He could see Thai standing there, watching what he had caused. When Thornton got back to the dunes, he and Norris started setting up their defensive perimeter for the coming battle. "We put the stupid shit, Thai, at our rear for security," remembers Thornton. "We didn't want him doing anything more that could kill us."

By now, a firefight with the fifty NVA soldiers had begun. "I wasn't too worried about these fifty," Mike says. "Because they were so exposed, we quickly killed eighteen of them." Tommie Norris immediately began working the radio to get ship gun support.

The North Vietnamese thought they were fighting a larger force than they were, because Thornton was returning fire from as many different positions as he could. The Vietnamese stopped their advance until reinforcements could get there. During this short lull, Thornton went back to make sure everyone was okay. "We were in a world of trouble," Thornton admits.

He knew that, when the reinforcements came, the attack would continue. Looking to his right, just beyond the marsh, he saw at least seventy more NVA soldiers coming. Norris was on the radio just behind Thornton, trying to arrange for ship's guns to help them out of the mess. But they didn't even know where they were.

"I moved up again, firing my machine gun and the rockets we had brought," remembers Thornton. "Hand grenades were being exchanged. One kept coming back at me as I picked it up and threw it, and I actually threw it two times before it finally went off and filled my back with shrapnel." Enemy soldiers started making it into the SEALs' perimeter, and hand-to-hand combat began.

The Vietnamese were moving forward in force. There was a final sand dune about four hundred yards behind the SEALs. Norris told Thornton to move to it with Thai and Quan. Norris and Dang would cover. Before Thornton left, a quick and desperate interrogation of the beach guard whom Thornton had earlier rifle-butted in the head revealed to the SEALs their exact beach location. Norris quickly radioed this position to the cruiser *Newport News*, and said, "Give us five minutes and then fire for effect." The beach would be blown away.

Thornton followed Norris's instructions and ran with Quan and Thai to the back dune while Norris and Dang covered. Thornton could see the NVA attackers coming over the dunes behind him, and then he saw Dang running to him, yelling, "Dowie is dead! Dowie is dead!" "Dowie" was the Vietnamese name for "Tommie."

Thornton wouldn't believe it. He hadn't seen it personally; and until he did—as far as he was concerned—Tommie Norris was still alive. A SEAL never left another SEAL behind, dead or alive. "I knew what I had to do," says Thornton. "I was coming back with Tommie or I wasn't coming back."

Thornton started running back into the enemy attackers. "I jumped into Tommie's bunker and saw Tommie unconscious with half his face gone," remembers Thornton. Two guys jumped over the edge of the dune. Thornton immediately shot them. Then he threw Norris over his shoulder and started running backward while firing his gun from the waist.

Just then, the *Newport News* started firing its eight-inch rounds into the beach. The first shell exploded knocking Thornton forward. Norris's limp body was blown off Thornton's shoulders. "I grabbed him, picking him up. He opened his remaining eye and said, 'Mike, buddy.' This was the first I knew he was still alive." By now, Dang and Quan could see what Thornton was doing. They came out of their sand dune, firing their guns at the NVA attackers. The bombardment from the cruiser was now devastating the beach. "I got behind the dune with Tommie," remembers Thornton. "That beach bombardment was what saved us."

Thai had already left the team and was in the water, swimming out. Dang and Quan stayed with Thornton and Norris, and started yelling, "Mike, what we do? What we do?" Thornton responded, "We swim. We swim." With Norris still under his arm and with shrapnel wounds in his back and face, Thornton started running backward to the beach with the rest of the team. They fired their guns as they went.

It was a full three hundred yards before they hit the water. Many of the Vietnamese were face down on the sand, trying to avoid being blown away by the ship's bombardment. "We made it to the water and I dragged Tommie in," Thornton recalls. The firefight had been going on for four hours now, and the team was getting tired.

"Hitting the water, I wrapped my arms around Tommie," remembers Thornton. "I threw my AK-47 over my shoulder and threw my M-16 away. Dang and Quan kept firing their weapons and backed into the water."

The men started swimming out, while some NVA attackers made their way into the water after them. Holding guns over their heads, the attackers fired at the escaping SEALs. Without explanation, the *Newport News* stopped its barrage of fire. This allowed the full force of the remaining North Vietnamese soldiers to run to the ocean's edge and wade into the water, firing their rifles, too. Bullets were splashing all around the escaping SEALs.

Only Quan—a little guy, less than five feet tall—had not been hit. When a big wave threw him back toward shore, he was exposed. The right side of his buttocks was shot off. He barely made it back into the water and, with his painful injury, swam out to Thornton and grabbed his arm.

Thornton's powerful breast strokes pulled Norris and Quan out deeper into the ocean, and finally beyond the NVA beach fire. Only then did Thornton inflate Norris's life vest. Norris partially woke up. He looked at Mike Thornton—not quite sure where he was—and asked if everyone had made it out. Before Thornton had a chance to answer yes, Norris was unconscious again.

The team swam for the next two and a half hours—straight out and then south, looking for rescue. Thornton put battle dressings on Norris's wounds. Half his face was gone, and so was part of his head. He was bleeding; and when he wasn't unconscious, he was delirious. Thornton was surprised Tommie Norris was still alive.

By now, all but one person on the SEALs' extraction group thought the entire team was dead. Woody Woodruff was a SEAL who wouldn't give up. He hoped the escaping SEALs had made it into the water. He kept patrolling up and down the coast—looking, in case they did.

Thornton felt very alone with his wounded team hanging onto him in the dark ocean. After what seemed an eternity, though, he did see Woody's rubber boat. At first, he wasn't sure if it was American or enemy, but he started swimming toward it. When he saw the boat was American, he fired his AK-47 into the air.

The rubber boat moved up to the team, and Norris was quickly pulled over the side. Dang and Quan followed. Thornton was so exhausted he had trouble getting into the boat, but he finally made it. Immediately, Thornton radioed the *Newport News* and identified himself. The men were rushed straight to the cruiser where a chair was thrown down to pull Norris up. By the time Thornton made it to the deck, a doctor was already working on Norris. The Vietnamese officer, Thai, had been picked up earlier, and he was already on the deck when Thornton arrived. "I felt like shooting him," remembers Thornton. "He had given away our position, which almost killed us, and he left the team while we were under fire."

A helicopter from Da Nang came for Tommie Norris. Because so few Americans were left in Vietnam and there wasn't a neurosurgeon in the whole country, Norris was sent to Clark Air Force Base in the Philippines. He didn't make it to an operating table for more than twenty-four hours, but he survived and lived to thank the man who saved his life.

"I received the Medal because I did my job," says Mike Thornton. "This was a job I was trained for and, as a SEAL, was expected to do. I also did something for a person who would have done the same thing for me. I didn't need to be rewarded for that."

In October 1973, Mike Thornton received this country's highest honor, the Congressional Medal of Honor. Attending that ceremony was Tommie Norris, who later received his own Medal of Honor for a downed-pilot rescue mission in North Vietnam. Attending *that* ceremony was the man who made it all possible: Mike Thornton.

15.

THOMAS G. KELLEY

His Duty

Some actions leading to a Medal of Honor combine a high sense of duty and responsibility with a high level of military training. Throughout Tom Kelley's naval career, he learned his jobs well and became proficient. Later, when combat situations presented themselves, Kelley was ready. His "combat reflexes"—developed through years of naval training—had clearly prepared him for what needed to be done. And he did it.

Thomas G. Kelley
Lieutenant Commander, U.S. Navy
Ong Muong Canal,
Kien Hoa Province, Republic of Vietnam
15 June 1969

The mighty battleship USS *Missouri* was known for its many great acts of service to the country, including supplying the platform for the Japanese surrender that ended World War II. One of its lesser known feats occurred in the late 1940s when a young boy named Tom Kelley visited her decks, saw her smartly dressed sailors wearing bell-bottom uniforms, and thought that someday he would become a sailor just like them. He did, eventually adding this country's highest military honor to a long and proud naval tradition.

Thomas Kelley was born in Boston, Massachusetts, on May 13, 1939. He went to Boston College High School and then to Holy Cross College. "I thought about going to Harvard, but my mother thought it would make me quit going to Mass," remembers Kelley.

Kelley didn't join the ROTC at Holy Cross College: the ROTC wouldn't take him because of his poor 20/200 eyesight. But when he graduated on June 15, 1960, he was sworn in. He began Officer Candidate School (OCS) in Newport, Rhode Island.

"I wasn't one of those ninety-day wonders' where a civilian was changed into an officer in just three months," says Kelley. "It took me 107 days, and I knew I was going to be another John Paul Jones."

Just a week before Kelley was to be commissioned, his father and greatest hero—John Basil Kelley—died suddenly of a heart attack. "He was only sixty-two years old and such a good, kind, solid man," remembers Kelley. "Everyone looked up to him." Because of his father's death, Kelley left Officer Candidate School for home and missed commissioning with his class.

It was a sad time for Kelley. His father had been very proud of his son the future naval officer. "Kids do things to make their parents proud, and I no longer had my father to look to," says Kelley. "His death took the wind out of my sails. It was the first big disappointment in my life."

His father's death made Kelley even more committed to live up to his father's expectations. The young sailor felt obliged—for the memory of his father—to do the best job be could.

Kelley's first assignment was aboard a converted LST (landing ship tank) affectionately referred to by the crew as the "Rust Bucket." An LST is an ocean-going ship that can carry vehicles and troops on beach-landing operations. Stationed in Charleston, South Carolina, the ship's mission during peacetime was to repair minesweepers. Kelley became the ship's operations and weapons officer.

Because of its peacetime mission, the ship had a large repair department. In fact, this ship had more than the usual share of very experienced warrant officers. The men had come up through the ranks as carpenters, machinist mates, and electricians. These men were commissioned because they were so good at these trades. In fact, there were four or five men on the ship with twenty-five to thirty years in the Navy, and there were none better at what they did. They were also twice as old as Kelley . . . and Kelley, the new ensign, was supposed to be their boss!

As Kelley puts it, "Here I was—a young officer right out of college. And I was going to show these guys how a Navy ship is going to operate?!" Within a day or two, the warrant electrician, Mr. Cranford, took Kelley aside and said, "Hey kid, I got a deal for you." Kelley hadn't really expected an old salt of a sailor to address him as "sir," anyway—the way superior officers were usually addressed.

Cranford continued, "The old man [the captain] just put out the word that us old warrant officers have to start standing watches on the bridge to become qualified as deck officers. We've never been topside in our twenty-five years in the Navy. You learned all that deck-officer crap in OCS, didn't you?" Kelley answered, "Yes, Sir"—not thinking that superior officers didn't address their warrant officers with "sir." Cranford went on, "If you can help us get qualified as watch standing officers, then we warrants will show you how to be a naval officer." Then he looked at Kelley with those steel eyes that had seen battle in World War II, and the young ensign felt Cranford's gaze burn right through him. Kelley stammered, "Yes, sir."

A deal was struck, and Kelley's real officer training began.

"I helped the warrants become deck officers, and those guys taught me how to be an officer," Kelley remembers. "I learned from them what it takes to be a leader of men. I learned it not so much from what they said, but from what they did." Kelley stayed with his teachers for two years. Men like Machinist Leroy Hagey, Carpenter Ben Risher, Electrician Fred Aldridge, Electrician Cranford, and the ship's repair officer, Mr. York—who had been in the Navy for thirty years—took Kelley under their wings. Eventually, all the warrants became qualified deck officers and Kelley became a naval officer.

During the two years on the Rust Bucket, Kelley learned the importance of teamwork. He learned that in the Navy you rely on your shipmates in every aspect of day-to-day life. You learn to trust your shipmates, and they learn to trust you. Without trust, nothing gets accomplished. "Those years on that old repair ship were very enlightening and educational for me," says Kelley. "My most significant learning occurred during this time."

Kelley remembers the ship's young supply officer named Todd Hunt. Hunt was a pretty studious guy who kept a low profile. He always seemed to be in his room, writing. It turned out he was writing a novel titled *The Ship with a Flat Tire*, which was later published. "The novel was a funny 'Mr. Roberts' kind of thing," says Kelley. "But if you knew our ship, you would know it was a pretty accurate portrayal. It was in the bookstores and libraries, and we all got a kick out of reading it."

The most important military situation that occurred during Kelley's early years in the Navy was the Cuban Missile Crisis in 1962. All the ships on the East Coast were put to sea on short notice, with orders to steam toward the Caribbean. Kelley's ship anchored in Puerto Rico and waited. Kelley remembers, "We were part of the supporting force for the blockade. I remember being very scared about a nuclear confrontation, but we really didn't have too much time to think about it."

During this time, Kelley developed his love for the Navy. After his two years on the Rust Bucket, he applied for destroyer school. Kelley believed that more training would broaden his experience and get him assigned to some of the more capable ships in the Navy. He got turned down. He was told he didn't have sufficient experience on destroyers to go to destroyer school. Because destroyer school would give him destroyer experience, he wasn't quite sure about this reasoning. But Kelley was starting to understand the Navy.

Armed with his destroyer school rejection, Kelley went back to the Navy and asked for a department head assignment on a destroyer—a choice position usually sought by officers graduating from destroyer school. Appropriately illogical, of course, this request resulted in his assignment as operations officer on the USS *Stickell*. It was 1963, and Kelley was continuing to learn.

When the USS *Stickell* shipped out for a European cruise, Kelley was excited. "I probably brought aboard that ship a lot more competence than I knew I had," says Kelley. "I was a better naval officer than I thought, because of my experience on the Rust Bucket. Even without the benefit of destroyer school, I had a job which graduates of destroyer school would have loved." Kelley was getting older and becoming an excellent naval officer. The lessons from the old salty warrant officers were staying with him.

In January 1966, the USS *Stickell* was sent to Southeast Asia as part of the second group of East Coast ships deploying to Vietnam. This experience opened a whole new world to Kelley. He saw airplanes with young pilots take off from aircraft carriers and not return. He listened to rescue attempts on the radio, and heard both successes and failures. The USS *Stickell* fired guns in support of troops on the beaches. For the first time, Kelley started to realize the seriousness of his job and what it really means to be in the Navy. "This experience off the coast of Vietnam made me mature faster in three months than over the previous six years," recalls Kelley.

Sitting offshore at no personal risk, Kelley came to the sobering realization that American men no different from him were getting killed just a few miles onshore. Some of the guys going in there were making it, and some weren't. Kelley decided that at his first opportunity he would volunteer to serve "in country." As he says, "It made me feel uncomfortable sitting safely on that ship while other people, just like me, were going through hell. I felt guilty and I felt I could contribute."

Seven months later, when Kelley returned from the Western Pacific, he was assigned to shore duty in Newport, Rhode Island. One of his old shipmates, also on shore duty, had just returned from a year in Da Nang, and he filled Kelley's ears with stories of what it was like. This made Kelley even more anxious to get back there and involved firsthand. He wondered how he would react to combat.

In the summer of 1968, Kelley was finally given an assignment to Vietnam. He was happy to go, but he was also scared. His assignment was duty with the Mobile Riverine Force on the Mekong Delta. This was dangerous work. His squadron's mission was to carry troops back and forth in small boats, inserting and extracting them from the riverbanks—just like the helicopters dropping off and picking up troops farther inland.

Kelley was assigned as the chief staff officer in River Assault Squadron 9 (RAS-9). RAS-9 was a unit of four hundred men. Kelley was a lieutenant and the second in command. The squadron had fifty boats that were primarily converted LCM-6 World War II crafts. Each of these craft could carry one platoon of thirty to forty men and a crew of five sailors commanded by a very competent E-5 or E-6.

It was a great honor to be an enlisted man in charge of one

of these boats. It was a tremendous responsibility for such a man, and the Riverine Force experience gave people commands that they could never have had otherwise.

Kelley spent the first several months of his RAS-9 tour in an administrative role. There were two divisions, with twenty-five boats and two hundred men in each division. Five staff officers oversaw both divisions, with Kelley serving as the chief of staff.

Some missions required all fifty boats carrying six hundred soldiers. On these missions, the squadron commander and Kelley would also be on the boats. Otherwise, his job was to make sure the guys got fed, clothed, and transferred when they needed to be. Kelley's job was administrative in nature; the commander was the real warrior. So, Kelley kept his job in proper perspective. He realized that somebody had to do the administrative work. He tried to make sure that things were done properly.

As the year went on, Kelley developed a stronger desire to be a division commander and take on a combat leadership role. He got his wish when he was assigned to command the 152nd Riverine Assault Division, in April 1969.

"This assignment was a great opportunity for me, and it was the reason I had come to Vietnam," recalls Kelley. "I now had ultimate responsibility for the welfare of two hundred men and twenty-five boats. I answered to an O-5 squadron commander."

The new assignment meant leaving his shipmates at RAS-9 and getting to know a whole new group of people in the 152nd Division. But it was also the opportunity Kelley wanted: he could finally focus his energy and attention on fighting the war and operating with the boats on a daily basis. "I no longer had the paperwork or the administrative details, and I felt much closer to my men than when I had been chief staff officer," says Kelley. "This was important to me because, now, I felt more a part of the team."

In January 1969, Kelley was sent with a six-boat group on a special operation called "Giant Slingshot." This operation was intended to interdict Vietcong troops and supplies coming down two rivers from Cambodia, northwest of Saigon. The assignment was truly independent duty, because Kelley and his men were off by themselves for about six weeks. It was also a great opportunity for Kelley to learn the operational aspects of his new job. "Our six boats patrolled and supported the Army," says Kelley. "We also provided security for the area's small villages and towns. During this time, I became much more aware of the human toll of war."

Early in this mission, Kelley and his Riverines pulled up to a riverbank at a small town when two little children—a six-year-old girl and her three-year-old brother—came wandering up to the boats. Kelley discovered, through an interpreter, that these kids didn't have a mother or a father because both had been killed in the war. Initially scared of the Riverines, the children were so starved for affection that, when the men responded to them, they just fell into the sailors' midst and became part of the group.

The Riverines adopted these kids for the next several weeks. When Kelley and his boats went on patrol, the kids would stand on the riverbanks, crying while they waved goodbye. But when the boats came back, the kids would be standing there waving and smiling: their adopted parents had returned.

"These children didn't have food," remembers Kelley. "They also didn't have shelter to sleep in at night; they always slept with us on the boats. We gave them food and candy, but we were amazed at how self-sufficient these two little kids were. It was incredible how the little six-year-old girl could take care of her three-year-old brother way out in the tullies of Hiep Hoa.

"They were two of the most beautiful children I had ever seen. I would love to know they were survivors because, when we left, we had to leave them there. This experience taught us how helpless the real victims—the very young and the very old—are, in war."

After this mission, Kelley came back to his division assignment, where operations were relatively quiet for a few weeks.

He continued daily patrols until mid-June 1969, when the area of operations for the division shifted to a new location. This was true "Indian country."

On Friday, June 13, 1969, Kelley's division took a large Army unit down the river. "We had about five hundred troops on our twenty boats, and our mission was to insert these troops on the riverbank," remembers Kelley. While en route to the landing area, the boats came under heavy enemy fire. Kelley tried to get away, but those old boats were built for power—not speed— and they couldn't go faster than six knots. Their guns blazed back at the enemy, but still the Vietcong gunners continued the attack.

On this morning, one of the Vietcong gunners was either very good or very lucky: he put a rocket-propelled grenade round directly into the well deck of one of the troop-carrying boats. This single grenade killed or seriously wounded forty Army soldiers.

Kelley recalls, "I was devastated by the disaster. My job was to make sure these guys were transported safely, and a bunch of them got killed under my command." It was one of the worst days in the history of the Mobile Riverine Force in Vietnam. With this disaster, the mission was aborted. The boats went back to base.

The whole next day was spent planning a return to the area. The Riverines wanted to go back; and they were ready on Father's Day, Sunday, June 15, 1969. "I hadn't been very good about going to church since I had been in country," remembers Kelley. "But for some reason, I went to Mass that morning before the mission. Afterwards, my division of twenty boats took off, heading for the same landing area which killed all those guys on Friday."

This time the Riverines had two Navy helicopters with them for close support. These helicopters scouted ahead of the riverboat column and even made a successful landing at the initial troop-insert location. Kelley kept up a pattern of dropping off the troops, moving down the river a few kilometers, then picking them up again, throughout the day.

"We repeated this operation two more times with our five hundred infantry troops," remembers Kelley. "Finally, we were told to make one more insertion at a point very deep in Indian country." As fate would have it, about this time the helicopters were recalled for a higher priority mission, and whatever sense of security Kelley may have had all but dwindled away. "It was kind of weird," says Kelley. "Even though we hadn't been hit yet, I expected to be hit on this last insertion."

Kelley dropped off the troops and moved a couple of kilometers down the river to the final pickup point of the day. So far, the Americans had not received any enemy contact at all, but it was like waiting for the other shoe to drop. "As the troops were coming back aboard the boats at this final pickup, all hell broke loose from the bank opposite the pickup area," remembers Kelley. "Intense enemy fire was coming from a large area." The river was about one hundred meters wide at this point.

When the firing began, the troops hurried aboard the boats. One of the last boats on the beach reported to Kelley that its ramp's hydraulic system had been hit and wasn't working. The ramp was stuck down, leaving it completely exposed to enemy fire. Kelley remembers that someone from the disabled boat was yelling on the radio, "We can't get the ramp up! We're being hit!"

The boat's crew started winching the ramp up by hand. Until the ramp was up, the boat couldn't leave the shore to join the column of other boats; it would have flooded and sunk. The enemy started concentrating its fire on the exposed boat filled with troops.

As the commander of the division, Kelley had only one thought in mind. He needed to keep the intense fire away from the exposed boat. He knew a direct hit could kill forty more men, so he immediately positioned his own boat directly in the line of fire between the enemy on the opposite bank and the exposed boat. He ordered the men in the other boats to open up with everything they had.

"I never dreamed I would get hit," recalls Kelley. "It never even crossed my mind. But all of a sudden, the strangest thing happened. There was this tremendous noise and concussion. An explosion occurred. I felt like I had been completely swallowed up." A rocket-propelled grenade had detonated on a pipe about a foot from Kelley's head. The force of the explosion knocked him from the perch of his boat between two gun tubes and sent him flying through a shaft about eight feet to the bottom of the boat. Half his face was gone, and he couldn't see. Kelley had been talking on two radios—using handsets—prior to getting hit. And when he fell, the handsets stayed in his hands.

"I had no sensation of time or place, but I could hear," remembers Kelley. "I could hear the gunfire, and I could hear the frantic voice of my boat captain shouting into his radio that I had been killed. This news of my death kind of shook me up and jolted me back to reality." Instinctively, Kelley managed to yell into both handsets, "I'm not dead! I'm still here! We're still fighting and we're going to get out of here!" Kelley gave orders to his boat captain, who had come to his assistance: "Keep firing the guns and don't move the boat." Then Kelley yelled into his radio handset at the beached boat, "Get that goddamn ramp up!"

The boat captain took over and started relaying Kelley's orders. The crew of the boat on the beach finished raising their ramp by hand. They started moving toward the column of boats that was forming in the river and was firing furiously at the enemy guns on the opposite shore. By now, enemy gunfire was being matched by the Riverine's return fire. "Everyone was still shooting like a son of a gun," says Kelley. When the last boat moved into the column, the boats started out of there as quickly as they could.

The pain from Kelley's wounds was getting worse. He was told that his boats had made it out and that everybody was okay. But it looked like Kelley himself was dying. An evacuation helicopter was called. Initially refusing evacuation, he later consented when his boats made it another few kilometers down the river. "My guys put me on a stretcher," recalls Kelley. "They told me they could handle it on their own. I was flown out, and everyone got back safely."

Thinking back, Kelley says, "This was my unit under fire. If a captain on the bridge of a ship sees enemy guns shooting his stern, he's not going to say, 'Well, he's not shooting at me. I'm not going to worry about it.' He's going to do something about it, just like I did."

Kelley was first taken to a jungle MASH unit where he remembers a doctor saying, "I don't think this fellow is going to make it." Kelley opened his remaining eye, looked at the doctor and replied, "Oh, I'm okay." That's the last thing Kelley remembers for several weeks. During this time he had seizures and was in a deep coma. The doctor was almost right.

Three weeks later, Kelley was transferred to a hospital in the States. He stayed for several months. The right side of his face and skull was remade of plastic. "When I woke up after being out for three weeks, I felt great, and I feel great to this day," Kelley says. "One eye is gone, but my body and mind are okay. Frankly, I have felt terrific ever since I woke up that day, three weeks after my injury. This has to be a miracle."

Kelley continues, "The Navy continuously trains during peacetime so that in wartime, if a tough situation arises, you will react instinctively the way you are supposed to. The proper action becomes second nature. What I did, any other officer would have done in the same situation.

"Involvement in this action was very valuable for me. It taught me about myself, and it taught me I was able to do what was expected of me in a bad situation. I responded the way I was trained to respond, and this is satisfying to me. I was able to play a small part in minimizing casualties to other members of my team.

"I took my responsibilities seriously. I don't like to think about it—but if I was asked to give my life that day to make sure none of my men were killed, I would have done it."

To men like these, presidents present the Congressional Medal of Honor.

ABOUT THE AUTHOR

KENT DeLONG is the attending physician of the Congressional Medal of Honor Society. He has a private medical practice in internal medicine with an emphasis in preventive and addictive medicine. He is a member of the board of DeLong International Inc., and has published numerous articles on commodities, addiction, and military history.